# THOUGHTS

ON THE

# FUTURE CIVIL POLICY

OF

# AMERICA.

BY

JOHN WILLIAM DRAPER, M.D., LL.D.,

PROFESSOR OF CHEMISTRY AND PHYSIOLOGY IN THE UNIVERSITY OF NEW YORK;
AUTHOR OF A "TREATISE ON HUMAN PHYSIOLOGY"
AND OF A
"HISTORY OF THE INTELLECTUAL DEVELOPMENT OF EUROPE."

FOURTH EDITION.

NEW YORK:
HARPER & BROTHERS, PUBLISHERS,
FRANKLIN SQUARE.
1875.

# PREFACE.

In a work on "The Intellectual Development of Europe," published in 1863, I showed that the historical progress of the nations of that continent illustrates the fact that social advancement is as completely under the control of natural law as is the bodily growth of an individual.

It was my intention in that work to limit the application of the principles employed to the case of Europe, but it is plain that they may equally be made to apply to the case of America.

Last winter, at the request of the New York Historical Society, I gave a course of four lectures for the purpose of showing that application.

The favor with which my work on Europe had been received, a great many editions, reprints and translations, of it having been called for in a short time, was again exhibited in the case of these lectures, and I became satisfied that it was desirable to give them a more permanent form.

Selecting, therefore, some of the more prominent principles thus presented, I design to show in this work their bearing on certain questions of great political interest in America. The lectures delivered before the Historical Society are here, of course, very much extended, the amount of matter having been almost quadrupled, and many new topics introduced.

Perhaps at the present moment, when the Republic has reached one of those epochs at which it must experience important transformations, it may not be inopportune to direct attention to the effects of physical agents and laws on the advancement of nations. We are too prone to depreciate their influence.

The aim of all science is prevision—the foretelling of the future. Historical foresight is not denied to man. As the Astronomer, from recorded facts, deduces the laws under which the celestial bodies move, and then applies them with unerring certainty to the prophesying of future events, so may the Historian, who relies on the immutability of Nature, predict the inevitable course through which a nation must pass.

To appreciate the working of some of those natural laws in the case of America, to divine the future tendencies of the Republic, to extract from the observations we make rules for national conduct—these are the objects to which the following pages are devoted.

New York, 1865.

---

## PREFACE TO THE SECOND EDITION.

A very large edition of this work has been exhausted in the course of a few weeks, and a second one is called for. For this mark of public approval I return my sincere thanks.

In this edition I have not thought it desirable or necessary to make any changes, except a few typographical corrections.

New York, *October*, 1865.

# CONTENTS.

## CHAPTER III.

### ON THE POLITICAL FORCE OF IDEAS.

## CHAPTER IV.

### ON THE NATURAL COURSE OF NATIONAL DEVELOPMENT.

# THOUGHTS

ON

# AMERICAN CIVIL POLICY.

---

## INTRODUCTION.

At the close of the Civil War, which has ended in the military vindication of the Great Republic, the minds of thoughtful men naturally turn to the Future. An Imperial power has come into existence before our eyes. It rivals—perhaps, indeed, it already excels—in warlike resources the ancient monarchies of Europe. There is before it a career of unparalleled grandeur, a splendid history, to be wrought out on a greater scale than that of Rome.

What topics, then, are more worthy of public attention than those with which American statesmanship will now necessarily be called upon to deal? With what else can the American reader, who has faith in the Destiny of his Nation, more profitably occupy himself? There are political problems of surpassing importance, for which solutions must now be found.

Having been occupied for many years in the study of the Intellectual Development of Europe, I have had occasion to observe the manner in which many of these problems have been solved on that continent. There are principles specially applicable to each nation, which guide it in its determinations, and settle the course of its life.

Some of these principles I propose now to point out, selecting from many topics the four following:

Influence of Climate,

Effects of Emigration,

Political Force of Ideas,

Natural Course of National Development,

and making these serve as a framework for the convenient presentation of those principles.

# CHAPTER I.

## ON THE INFLUENCE OF CLIMATE.

*Commencing with the statement that Nations, like all the forms of life, are transitory, the physical influences that originate and destroy those forms are considered. And since plants and animals are found to change helplessly under such influences, they are therefore illustrations of the control of* UNIVERSAL LAW. *A special inquiry is made as to the effects of Climate on the skin and skull of man, and on his physical and intellectual powers.*

*Then follows a brief topographical description of the United States; the Climate effects, North and South, are considered, and the conditions necessary to insure stability in the political institutions of the country are pointed out. The general inferences are illustrated by historical cases, as those of Egypt and Asia.*

*The main conclusion brought into relief is, that* PERSONAL LOCOMOTION *can check the effects of Climate. The importance of that locomotion in the development of the American Republic, and the necessity of legislation to encourage and secure it, are insisted upon.*

NATIONS, like individual men, are born and die—an unpalatable truth, for each tries to hide from itself the contemplation of its final day. Each also amuses itself with the delusion that, whatever may be the hapless lot of others, there is an immortal future in store for it. But what does the inexorable hand of History write? Rome, Macedon, Persia, Assyria, Egypt, all are gone.

The waves of the ocean spring up, we know not where or why. They come careering past us, the very emblems of resistless power. They subside and are lost among other succeeding waves. In like manner, on the vast sea of human life, Empires mysteriously emerge. They raise their ephemeral forms conspicuously high, overwhelming whatever stands in the way of their march. They also subside and are lost, but the unfathomed abyss of humanity still remains.

To the infinite expanse of the ocean belongs endless duration. Its waves are only temporary. The forces that have impelled them into existence are soon expended; an inevitable disappearance awaits them. The material of which they are composed may be eternal, but they themselves are only vanishing forms.

Vanishing forms! Such, too, are Nations emerging from the mass of humanity.

Then it might seem to be of trifling moment to concern ourselves with the study of any one of them. And so indeed it is, if we rise to the most elevated point of view that history can occupy. No isolated fact is of any intrinsic value in itself. It is its connection with other facts that gives it all its worth. No sound, whatever its quality may be, can ever of itself yield music; that arises from the well-ordered sequence of sounds. We only become conscious of historical harmony through a presentment of successive nations, varying in their form, their strength, their duration.

With what a solemn emphasis does the Past impress upon us its monition that national life is thus, in the necessity of circumstances, transitory! How vain it is to close our eyes to the portentous lesson, to refuse to read what is written in the Book of Destiny! How vain to try to persuade ourselves that, though all other things in the world are disappearing, we are to be immortal! Permanence may belong to humanity, but not to those forms into which, here and there at intervals, humanity has been forced. A succession of Nations is the consequence of the life of the race, being manifestations of the varying activity of groups of men. Life is the active, existence the passive state. Life is evanescent, existence is enduring.

Such groups of men, thus with an inevitable fate before them, may well desire, as does the individual man, to postpone as long as possible their end. They may legitimately seek to enjoy their existence while it lasts—nay, more, to make it memorable.

The analogy between the life of an Individual and of a Nation arises from a similarity in their constitution. In the individual there must be unceasing changes in the component parts. The appearance of permanence is altogether an illusion. Physicians sometimes say that the body changes completely in seven years. In truth, it changes far more quickly than that. The particles of which it is composed are continually becoming effete. They must be removed, and new ones introduced in their stead. Such replacements are going on from the moment of birth to that of death; they occur by night as well as by day; during sleep as well as when we are awake. This death of the constituent particles of a living being is called interstitial death. It is the very condition of life. It occurs in every part indifferently—in the soft textures, as in the muscles or nerves; in the hardest, as bone.

Energy of life depends altogether on the rapidity of these transmutations. No motion can be accomplished without the wasting away of substance. The foot can not take a step, the finger can not be lifted, the brain can not execute any intellectual act, without the death of a portion of its material. As such actions are more vigorous, the losses are greater. If, then, the body is to be maintained in an unimpaired condition, operations of renovation must needs be resorted to. On the removal of a particle that is dead, a new one must be ready to take its place. With rapidity and precision the process of transmutation goes on, and in a very short time a completely renovated structure, identical in form, but changed as to its constituents, is produced.

It is surprising on what an enormous scale these

transmutations are carried forward. An adult man, weighing not more than 140 pounds, requires to be supplied with nearly a ton and a half of material in the form of food, water, and air, in the course of every year, the larger portion of it being consumed in accomplishing these replacements. In the same period, the same weight, that is, a ton and a half of material, is dismissed from his system as dead or effete. The aspect of identity he presents is therefore altogether illusory. Particles are perpetually abandoning him, and new particles are being perpetually introduced. In a waterfall which retains its appearance for many years unchanged, the supply from above continually flows in, and the precipitated portions below glide finally and forever away. The waste is compensated by the supply. In no other manner can the transitory matter exhibit a permanent form. The waterfall is only a form which the flux of liquid assumes.

So in that collection of substance constituting man, or any animal, whatever may be its position, high or low, in the realm of life, there is a perpetual introduction of new material and a perpetual departure of the old.

And so, too, with Nations; they undergo unceasing change. The death of an individual in them corresponds to the death of a particle in the Individual. In the space of thirty or forty years—the period of a generation, as it is often called—a complete replacement has occurred. The men who were active have all been removed; succeeding men have occupied their places. If there has been a season of violent national exertion, such as of war, the substitution has gone on with greater rapidity. And yet, notwithstanding all this change, the nation may still exist with all its essential lineaments unimpaired. Like the man or the waterfall, it is only a transitory form.

Nor does the analogy between an Individual and a Nation end here. A similar, perhaps a more surprising parallelism is perceived when their modes of growth are considered, for not alone in the incidents of birth and death are they alike. As the former pursues his way through the successive stages of infancy, childhood, youth, maturity, old age, so, as history teaches, does the latter too. The Individual helplessly and in a predestined manner runs through these stages, being unable to modify their succession, or to accelerate or retard their occurrence. The Nation, also, in a like helpless and predetermined way, moves through the same inevitable career. An unavoidable destiny rules over the progress of both.

That transitory permanence, if such a contradictory expression may be used, which is equally seen in the Nation, the Individual, the Waterfall, depends on the invariability of external conditions. If they change, it also changes, and a new form is the result. In the waterfall, if the jutting ledge over which the waters rush should break suddenly away, or if some new obstacle interfere, the figure of the flowing sheet of liquid will be remodeled.

I repeat with emphasis the significant remark, that if external circumstances change, the transitory form will change with them; for it leads us by a ready step to the subject to which many of these pages are now to be devoted—the Influence of Climate on Man. To this I therefore hasten, premising, however, some preliminary thoughts and facts needful for its clear appreciation.

A rain-drop descends from the clouds: that simple phenomenon, like a thousand others we might consider, teaches us that there are two existences with which all exact science has to deal. They are Matter and Force. The substance of which the rain-drop consists might, if we chose, occupy our attention. We might dwell upon the nature, the properties, the constitution of water. And then, again, we might consider what is that power through the influence of which the drop has come down from the clouds, descending to the earth. Our books of Natural Philosophy teach us to call it gravitation: they speak of it as a Force. We see, therefore, the truth of the remark, that there are two things before us, Matter and Force.

Whence came that matter, that drop of water? Chemistry tells us that it was vaporized by the warmth of the sun from the ocean, perhaps many thousands of miles away. As an invisible steam it ascended through the air. Borne along by drifting winds, it came at length to a space where the atmosphere happened to be cooler, and, here condensing, lost the invisible and took on the visible form. Now it had become a portion of a cloud, ready to reflect the glories of the departing day. As a rain-drop it then fell to the ground, soaking through the earthy strata, to issue forth again in a gushing spring or fountain. In company with many others like itself, constituting a flowing rill that emptied into larger streams, it found through some river a return to the sea from which it came. After its many mutations, after all the vicissitudes it had undergone, an inevitable destiny awaited it—restoration to its original source.

So with the power that gently evaporated it from the sea, the power that in the winds drifted it from climate to climate, the power that made it fall to the ground, that carried it down the gently flowing current back to its native place, there was no deterioration, no decay. It might have assumed one form after another—motion, heat, and the like—but in its intrinsic nature it was altogether indestructible. It is the glory of modern science to have proved that Matter and Force are both imperishable.

For matter, see from the illustration here presented how, though it may pass from form to form, in what a returning circle it runs. For force it is the same. With predestined certainty both come back to their starting-point.

In the month of March the Sun crosses the Equator, dispensing his rays more abundantly over our northern hemisphere. Following in his train, a wave of verdure advances toward the pole. Trees, awaking from winter, assume their leafy ornaments. The vegetable world enters on a new period of growth. As autumn comes on, this orderly advance of light and life is followed by an orderly retreat, and in its turn the other hemisphere, the southern, presents the same beautiful appearance.

Whence came all these green leaves and tinted flowers, these seeds that are to furnish food for man? Not from the ground, as some persons think. The Omnipotent Sun, that central governor of our planetary system, obtains and condenses the needful material from the air. Under his genial influences a refined chemical operation is going on. He extracts from an invisible and noxious gas—the same that is expired from our lungs in the act of breathing, as useless and even poisonous to the system—that plastic material out of which the unnumbered beautiful plant-organs are composed. Plants are therefore nothing more than condensations from the Air, their parts being held together by Force that has been derived from the Sun—force that, as it were, is imprisoned in them, but ever ready to re-appear. Each year, in this manner, through that arch-chemic influence, a store of Matter and of Force is laid up, as we are now to see, for the animal world.

For, directly or indirectly, all animals find their nutrition in feeding on plants. Even for those called carnivorous, or flesh-feeders, the remark holds good. They feed on others that have fed on plants. The muscles, and fat, and nerve substance, nay, the very bone, all have come from the vegetable world.

Wherein is the imperious necessity that food thus composed and thus obtained should be used by man and other animals? It is for the double purpose of securing Matter and Force. The former, in being consumed, furnishes the latter.

We have already seen that an animal is only a transitory form, through which material substance is visibly passing. A scientific examination of its life must include two primary facts. It must consider whence and in what manner the stream of material substance has been derived, and whither it passes away. And since Force can not be created from nothing, and is in its very nature indestructible, it must determine from what source that which is displayed by animals has been obtained, in what manner it is employed, and what disposal is made of it eventually. The Force comes from the Sun, the Matter from the Air.

But how does all this wasted material, that has subserved its offices in animals, escape from them? To so great an extent by the breath, that, with certain exceptions needless to notice here, it may be said that the breathing of animals is essential to the growing of plants. We cast out into the atmosphere those inert products no longer useful to life. Plants then appropriate them under the influence of the Sun, and organize them again. And this brings us back to the same truth that was revealed to us by the drop of water. There is a cycle or revolution through which material particles suitable for organization incessantly run. At one moment they exist as inorganic combinations in the air or the soil, then as portions of plants, then as portions of animals, then they return to the air or the soil, once more to renew their cycle of movement. The metamorphoses feigned by the poets of antiquity have hence a foundation in fact; and the Vegetable and Animal, the organic and inorganic worlds, are indissolubly bound together. Plants form, animals destroy.

In this relation of the Plant and Animal worlds to each other, there is a condition too important to be overlooked. It is their mutual interbalancing. The sum total of the one must be exactly adjusted to that of the other. If either were permitted to acquire a superiority, it would impress upon the atmosphere a specific change. If animal life predominated, the quantity of carbonic acid would preponderate; if plant life, the quantity of oxygen. Now there is evidence the most copious, the most satisfactory, that for many thousands of years the relative quantity of these ingredients has remained unchanged. The atmosphere is to-day the same in composition that it was sixty centuries ago.

There must therefore have been during that long lapse of time a rigorous adjustment of the two forms of life to one another, neither being permitted to gain a superiority, but each minutely and exactly balanced to the other. I will not at present enter on a description of the simple manner in which this equipoise is accomplished, but will be content with the emphatic remark, that in the most conspicuous manner it indicates THE EXISTENCE OF CONTROLLING LAW.

The material which has flowed through the heart of man as blood, is transferred by breathing to the air, and aids in the formation of forest-trees and flowers. The Asiatics, with whom have originated all the varieties of religious creeds that have spread to any extent in the world, not unfrequently asserted a transmigration of souls. They would have been much nearer the truth had they believed in a transmigration of bodies. The coal that we burn is the remains of forests which in former ages were thronged with living things—forests that sprang, as do the trees with us, from gases that were formed by the respiration of animals, but of animals that are now all extinct.

Atmospheric air is then the grand receptacle from which all living things come, and to which they all return. It is the cradle of vegetable, the coffin of animal life. Made up as it is of atoms that have once lived, that have run through innumerable cycles of change, the aspect of purity it presents conceals too well its history. In its ethereal expanse are crowds of particles that have once blossomed as flowers, or participated in the pleasures and pains of animal life. Their former function discharged, they await their turn of re-organization, occupying themselves in transmitting the many-colored beams of light, or moving in vibration to musical sounds. A condition so tranquil suits well their former state and future destiny. In this general tomb the remains of wild beasts and of more ferocious men disappear, until the solar beams recall them to life and give them form again.

The daily rotation of the Earth on her axis determines periodic observances in the functions of organized beings, and fixes their times of activity and sleep. A similar result attends her yearly motion in her orbit. In our latitudes trees and plants awake at the coming of spring, and put forth their leaves and flowers, and then sink again into their annual slumber. Wild birds and beasts conform their habits to the progress of the seasons, at one time preparing to bring forth their young, at another anticipating with a provident foresight the coming winter. It is thus with those flocks of pigeons which in countless myriads seek the North in spring and return to the South in autumn; thus, also, with the vast herds of buffaloes in the West. The migrations of fishes that take place at given seasons, and which are connected with the well-being and wealth of nations, are determined by the occurrence of astronomical epochs. It is no explanation of these curious facts to say that they depend on other facts like themselves—that an animal sleeps by night because his prey is also asleep—that a fish migrates at those periods when his instincts tell him that the food on which he lives is abundant. If in any of these cases we pass from fact to fact, we uniformly come at last to the conclusion that all these incidents are under the control of astronomical events; that the Sun not only determines periods of awakening and sleep, of growth and decay, but that he controls and regulates the movements of animated beings all over the face of the Earth. His rays, falling perpendicularly, produce the luxuriant vegetation of tropical regions, and debilitate and enervate the human race. In the polar regions their obliquity suffers the ground to be always covered with snow, and makes those inhospitable countries almost without inhabitants. The trade winds also, blowing uninterruptedly for ages, carry toward the poles immense quantities of oxygen gas, which the green parts of plants throw into the atmosphere of the torrid zone. That oxygen is evolved by light and then disseminated by heat. In the sea the same influence which thus presides in the air is also at work. The Gulf Stream, issuing from the Mexican waters, with its temperature elevated by solar action, determines the distribution of the Atlantic fishes: the Northern whale avoids its offensive warmth, and on its sides shoals congregate which delight in a more genial heat. As it approaches the coasts of Europe, and spreads out into a fan-like form, the vapors that rise from it give forth their latent heat to the air, and moderate the climates of England and France. The coldness and sterility of corresponding latitudes in America are there replaced by a better temperature; and agriculture, the arts of life, science, and literature, have there reached their greatest perfection. This physical agent, thus eternally but invisibly continuing its operation, produces a thousand events in which its agency is only remotely traced: nor are those influences limited to mere physical results; they stand in connection with the progress of society and the evolution of mind. A full development of the reasoning faculty can only take place where physical circumstances conspire. Without the Gulf Stream, Newton would never have written his Principia, nor Milton Paradise Lost.

In these events, which strike us forcibly when we

thus trace them step by step from their origin to their results, we are prone, at a casual glance, to give too much weight to intervening influences, and forget the final cause. We may assert that, with returning seasons, periods of vegetation, and the distribution of plants and animals, astronomical occurrences likewise direct a thousand of those daily movements taking place in every part of the world. There is no gathered harvest, no desolating famine, that has not sprung from an immediate connection with them. In judging from a narrow circle of observation or from an imperfect experience, men are led to regard these as fortuitous affairs. In truth, they are brought about by unfailing and unchangeable causes. The breeze that for a little time distends a passing sail—the glimpse of light, which, issuing through some break in the clouds, for a moment shines upon it, were preordained from the beginning of things—they came in the resistless necessities of the case. If they had not occurred, the order of Nature had that instant ended. From century to century the Sun pours forth his undiminished stores of light and heat; the former out of inorganic material constructing molecules that are organized, and with them composing the myriads of vegetables destined to support animal life; the latter controlling the movements of inorganic things, dividing into climates the earth's surface, volatilizing water from the sea, setting the wind in motion, and directing the form, duration, and movement of the clouds. The primitive force at work producing these vital and meteorological phenomena undergoes no variation in intensity from year to year. It is therefore expended in producing the same amount of effect. For this reason, the droughts of one country are contemporaneous with the abundant showers of another; the famine threatening one place is compensated by harvests in another. As natural laws were never meant for individuals, but for universal action on systems and masses, we must take care that we are not misled in our interpretation of these incidental vicissitudes. Operating with unerring certainty and with unvarying force, the Sun carries on his plastic work, as the Earth in her daily rotations submits herself to his beams. From this it comes to pass that, though there may be variations in the lot of particular individuals or of particular nations, the common interests of all are protected, the common rights of all upheld. From the very beginning of things every class of variation has been determined — where particular climates shall fall, where particular temperatures shall be observed, what shall be the speed of vegetable growth, what tribe of animals shall be given — and the result remains fixed and invariable.

If we consider the successive races of organized beings, beginning from the lowest and passing to the higher tribes, it would seem as if the general idea under which Nature is acting is, as the more complex structures are evolved, to emancipate them from the direct control of external physical forces. The Vegetable Kingdom, unendued with locomotive powers, deriving its existence directly from external agents, is completely under their control. If the summer is too brilliant, or rains do not fall, a plant withers and dies. In the same manner, the lower races of animals have their existence determined by the action of physical causes: if these be favorable, they flourish; if unfavorable, they must submit to an inevitable lot. To tribes that are higher, to a certain extent the rigor of these laws is remitted, and a certain amount of independence allowed. The Lion can retire to a shade in the middle of the day; yet still he is held in a state of subjection, and instinctively submits to the operation of an overruling power, and is kept to the sands of his desert, from cool and temperate climates. The sunbeam is his chain. In man alone the emancipation is complete, for nature has committed a control of her forces to him. It matters not whether he be in the torrid zone or the frigid, he can temper the seasons by resorting to artifices of clothing or by the management of fire. He also can dissipate the darkness of night by artificial light, prolonging for many hours each day his active existence, and increasing his social enjoyments. Developed by civilization, he is no more a prey to the accidents of the seasons. If the harvests in his own country have failed him, he has created commerce, which brings him an abundance from distant places. Unlike inferior tribes, which instinctively aim at the result he so perfectly accomplishes, he does not wait upon Nature, but compels her to minister to him. Oppressed by hunger, fishes migrate in the sea, and innumerable flocks of birds direct their flight through the air; but civilized man, without calling into action his own locomotive powers, puts his arm across the globe and satisfies his wants.

But, though thus seemingly the master, man is really the dependant of physical agencies. The development of his intellect, which gives him a control over them, is, in truth, determined by them. To be satisfied of this, we have only to compare the effect of climates in the torrid, temperate, and frigid zones. We might appeal to individual experience as to the enervating effect of hot climates, or to common observation as to the great influence exercised by atmospheric changes, not only on our intellectual powers, but even on our bodily well-being. It is within a narrow range of latitude that great men have been born. In the earth's southern hemisphere not one as yet has appeared.

Not without reason have I in the foregoing pages

dwelt upon the control that physical conditions exert over living beings, irrespective of their position in the scale of nature. For it necessarily follows that, should any thing transpire to impress a change on those physical conditions, a reflected effect must instantly be perceived in the organic forms. They must change too. Now the knowledge we have acquired of the past history of the earth instructs us that her surface has passed through many modifications, and that her physical condition has altered in the slow course of time. Her geographical aspect has undergone many mutations; there are continents where the sea once was, there are oceans where there was dry land. In a remote antiquity, the composition of the atmosphere was not the same as it is now; it contained more carbonic acid, less oxygen gas. The enormous quantities of coal, myriads of tons in weight, now enveloped in the solid strata, once existed in the air. Separated therefrom by the action of the solar rays, the atmospheric pressure necessarily became less. For sixty centuries, as I have already remarked, no appreciable change of this kind has occurred; and hence it follows that a period of almost limitless duration, so far as our standard of time is concerned, must have elapsed before changes so vast could be completed. How slow the work, that has not perceptibly advanced in many thousand years! And just as the composition of the air and its pressure have in this gradual manner passed through vast mutations, so likewise has the heat of the globe. There was a time when the intrinsic heat—that is, that appertaining to the Earth itself—was so high, that the climate differences, such as we now observe, were altogether concealed. But as that intrinsic heat gradually escaped away, and the globe became cooler and cooler, climates began to emerge. Now in this instance, as in the preceding, we are absolutely certain that there has been no recognizable diminution in many thousand years. Astronomical considerations establish that; for, among other things, the day must have become shorter, which has not been the case. We see, again, herein through what a limitless period the history of the Earth extends.

Looking through that limitless vista, and bearing in mind the absolute control exerted by physical agencies over organic forms, on which we have been so strenuously insisting, what is it we should expect to see? The physical influences—warmth, and pressure, and composition of air, the distribution of land and sea, and a thousand other things, have changed. With them, animated nature must also have changed. In the dense and noxious atmosphere of the primeval times, quickly-respiring, hot-blooded animals could not possibly exist. Physiology teaches us that such conditions are absolutely incompatible with their life; and, in corroboration, Geology proves that they did not appear until after the purification of the atmosphere had been accomplished, and the natural conditions were in unison with their mode of life.

The slowness of such changes in natural conditions implies, therefore, slow changes in the tribes of plants and animals—that is, in all organic forms. The former stands in the attitude of a cause, the latter in the attitude of an effect. And in the same manner that in their succession, obediently to these principles, the successive groups of living things made their appearance, so, too, in obedience to these principles, numberless groups, whose conditions of life had become incompatible with the changed exterior conditions, were necessarily eliminated—that is, became extinct. Just as the Mastodon, which once roamed all over the American continent, disappeared, through inability to withstand the increasing rigor of the winter, so myriads of the inhabitants of the ocean, the land, the air, passed away. The extinction of species is a necessary natural incident.

It is sometimes objected, by those who have not duly weighed the vast body of evidence now bearing upon these points, that we are not authorized to assume such a prodigious period for the duration of the Earth as these facts seem to require. Whoever presses that objection must bear in mind that these conclusions depend not on the immature results of a single branch of science, but are enforced by the concurrent testimony of all. Astronomy, Physiology, Chemistry, Geology, bear a concordant evidence. It is not the part of wisdom to couple with a chronological fiction great moral considerations in which the well-being of humanity is concerned. They will share in the discredit attaching to its inevitable discomfiture.

In the past history of the Earth there have then been slow variations in the vegetable and animal kingdoms, caused by slow variations in the condition of external nature. Physical influences have modified organic forms. But now, if we rise to a higher point of view, and examine what has been the cause of the changes in those controlling influences themselves, what is it that we see? The operation of universal law! In the special instance that has been occupying our attention—the decline of the earth's heat—an effect which has carried with it the most prodigious modifications both among living and lifeless things, that decline has been going on under the resistless operation of a law capable of mathematical expression—a law absolutely independent, free from all possibility of change. Thus, when we pursue the scientific investigation of facts to the last accessible point, there uniformly emerges the conception, the idea of law—law ever-enduring, exhibiting no variation, but so operating that out of the invariable and eternal, the changeable and perishable spring forth.

We gather, therefore, a most important lesson from inquiries respecting the origin, maintenance, distribution, and extinction of animals and plants, their balancing against one another—from the variations of aspect and form of an individual man, as determined by climate—from his social state, whether in repose or motion—from the secular variations of his opinions, and the gradual dominion of reason. This lesson is, that the government of the world is accomplished by immutable law.

Such a conception commends itself to the intellect of man by its majestic grandeur. It makes him discern the eternal through the vanishing of present events, and through the shadows of time. From the life, the pleasures, the sufferings of humanity, it points to the impassive; from our wishes, wants, and woes, to the inexorable.

But, in thus ascending to primordial laws, and asserting their immutability, universality, and paramount control in the government of this world, there is nothing inconsistent with the free action of man. The appearance of things depends altogether on the point of view we occupy. He who is immersed in the turmoil of a crowded city sees nothing but the acts of men; and, if he formed his opinion from his experience alone, must conclude that the course of events altogether depends on the uncertainties of human volition. But he who ascends to a sufficient elevation loses sight of the passing conflicts, and no longer hears the contentions. He discovers that the importance of individual action is diminishing as the panorama beneath him is extending. And if he could attain to the truly philosophical, the general point of view, disengaging himself from all terrestrial influences and entanglements, rising high enough to see the whole globe at a glance, his acutest vision would fail to discern the slightest indication of man, his free will or his works.

In whatever direction we look, we may therefore expect to find proofs of the dominion of law. Even in those cases where the voluntary agencies of man might seem to interfere, vestiges of that dominion are obvious enough. For instance, are not the greatest number of crimes against persons and property among the inhabitants of river banks? Does not the period of maximum of crimes against persons coincide with that which is the minimum against property—that is to say, the summer season? As respects each individual, is it not well known that his tendency to crime is at first against property, and this reaches its maximum at about twenty-five years of age? In maturer life he substitutes stratagem for force. If brought up in a liberal profession, his tendency to crime is against persons, but that of the workman is against property. If we look from his premeditated sins to his venial oversights, we still find the same result. Of a million of letters put into the Post-office year after year, there will be a fixed number misdirected, and a fixed number on which he has neglected to put any address at all.

It is the same with the other sex. In France, the tendency of females to crime, when compared with that of men, is as 23 to 100. Their tendency to the perpetration of offenses against persons is less than that for offenses against property in the proportion of 16 to 26. It also is interesting to observe that their physical force, if compared with that of man, is as the same numbers. From these and other such considerations, statesmen who have paid attention to the subject have come to the conclusion that the morality of men and women is, if fairly estimated, about the same—a conclusion, it need hardly be said, very flattering to the vanity of the former, and therefore, in spite of the whispers of gallantry, we may accept it as substantially true.

I have descended to these paltry facts, and quoted these seemingly trivial numbers, for the purpose of bringing into clearer relief the cardinal doctrine that in individual life, in social life, in national life, every thing is influenced by physical agents, and is therefore under the control of law. Far from denying the operation of man's free will, I give to that great truth all the weight that can be desired; but then I affirm there is something that overrides, that forever keeps it in check.

If the reader will try a very simple physiological experiment upon himself, he will probably come to a clearer understanding of what is here meant. Let him execute with his right hand the motion he would resort to in winding a thread upon a reel. Then let him do the same thing with his left hand, only winding the opposite way. Are not these two contrary motions which he thus consecutively accomplishes thoroughly under his control? He wills to do either, and forthwith either is done. Both illustrate his voluntary power. But next let him try to do both—not successively, but simultaneously. Let him put forth all the strength of his determination. A free-will actor, he has now the opportunity of giving an illustration of his power. In the failure of repeated trials, he may discern what his voluntary determinations come to, and what they are really worth. He may learn from this simple experiment that there is something that over-controls him, and puts a limit to his power.

There are physiological laws that constrain society. There are physical boundaries beyond which society can not pass. There are ends that no human legislation can accomplish.

The publication of Humboldt's Essay on the Geography of Plants first forcibly drew the attention of thinking persons to the control of climate over vegetables. Under the equator, where the heat is greatest, the Palm-tree, with its coronet of leaves, the banana and luxuriant climbing plants, give to the landscape its tropical characteristics. Advancing to the north or to the south, where the temperature is somewhat lower, there are evergreen woods in which flourish the orange and myrtle. Still journeying farther, these are succeeded by a zone of deciduous trees, such as the oak and the chestnut, and here the great climbers of the tropics are replaced by the hop and the ivy. Beyond, in a cooler zone, is a belt of firs, larches, pines, and other needle-leaved trees; and this, as we advance to the pole, leads us through birches and mosses to the perpetually snow-covered ground where vegetation ceases.

So, in like manner, as Tourneforte observed, a similar zone distribution occurs on the sides of mountains; the plants, as we ascend to the snow-covered peaks, being analogous to those occurring in succession on the surface as we advance to the poles. He first detected this fact while ascending Mount Ararat, about the year 1700, having previously studied the surface distribution in traveling from the Levant to Lapland.

In both these distributions the regulating condition is the declining heat. That is the only cause common to the two cases. The temperature becomes lower as we travel toward the pole, or ascend the mountain's side.

Now, should any thing occur to occasion a change in this arrangement of climate zones, a corresponding movement would undoubtedly occur in the zones of plant distribution. Nay, more than that, species unable to stand the change would at once become extinct; or if it occurred very slowly, they might, by undergoing modifications, be accommodated to it or acclimatized. So heat not only arranges the distribution of vegetable forms on the face of the Earth, it can also determine their extinction or occasion their transformation.

The influence of such variations of temperature is seen when we examine particular plants in different localities. Thus the Virginia cherry attains a height of a hundred feet in the Southern States, but it is dwarfed to a shrub of not more than five feet at the Great Slave Lake. The Nasturtium, which is a woody shrub in warm climates, is a succulent annual in cold. From such facts we learn this all-important lesson—that organisms of every kind, so far from presenting any resistance to change, yield helplessly to the influences to which they are exposed. The value of this conclusion, in its application to the case of man, we shall soon see.

The aspect of man in color and form oscillates between two extremes. Submitted for a due time to a high temperature, he will become dark, or if to a low temperature, he will become fair. The form of the skull will also alter. No race is in a state of absolute unchangeability, or able successfully to maintain its present physiognomy, if the circumstances under which it lives undergo alteration. It holds itself ready with equal facility to descend to a baser or to rise to a more elevated state, in correspondence to those circumstances.

That climate does thus influence complexion is clearly illustrated by the natural history of the Jews. These men, indisputably derived from a common stock, have different colors in different countries. In the north of Europe they are fair, having blue eyes and red beards. As we trace them in their southeasterly distribution, their color deepens by degrees. In Palestine they have become tawny, in India of a deep brown, in Malabar almost black. I do not consider that the recent affirmation of the existence of two distinct Hebrew tribes, the auburn-bearded and the black-bearded, can be either historically or physiologically sustained. A still more general instance is offered by the race to which we belong, the Indo-European, which reaches from Hindostan to the British Isles. That this is one homogeneous family, derived from a common stock, is proved by the affinities of its various languages to the Sanscrit. In nearly all those various tongues, the family names, Father, Mother, Brother, Sister, Daughter, are the same respectively. A similar equivalence may be observed in a great many familiar objects—House, Door, Town, Path. It has been remarked that while this holds good for terms of a peaceful nature, many of those connected with warfare and the chase are different in the different languages. Such facts appear to prove that the emigrating column followed a nomadic and pastoral life. Many of the terms connected with such an avocation are widely diffused. This is the case with plowing, grinding, weaving, cooking, baking, sewing, spinning; with such objects as corn, flesh, meat, vestment; with wild animals common to Europe and Asia, as the bear and the wolf. So, too, of words connected with social organization—despot, rex, queen. The numerals from 1 to 100 coincide in Sanscrit, Greek, Latin, Lithuanian, Gothic; but this is not the case with 1000, a fact which has led comparative philologists to the conclusion that though, at the time of the emigration, a sufficient intellectual advance had been made to invent the decimal system, perhaps from counting upon the fingers, yet that it was very far from perfection. To the inhabitants of Central Asia the sea was altogether unknown; hence the branches of the emigrating column, as they diverged north and south, gave it different names.

But, though unacquainted with the sea, they were familiar with salt, as is proved by the recurrence of its name. The bread-corn of the North is called rye, that of the South rice. Nor is it in the vocabularies alone that these resemblances are remarked; the same is to be said of the grammar.

Of this homogeneous family of men, the Indo-European, the complexion in the northwest is light, but it darkens toward the southeast of India; and, as if to guide us to the operating cause, this uniform deepening of the tint is broken through here and there as we cross regions more elevated above the sea, and therefore having a lower temperature. The inhabitants of the Caucasus and of the elevations of the Himmaleh Mountains are as light as the Southern Europeans, and there very frequently is seen the auburn-bearded and blue or gray eyed man.

As plants may be modified by heat, so, too, may men. The Roman authors bear their concurrent testimony to the fact that, twenty centuries ago, the inhabitants of Britain, Gaul, and Germany were red-haired and blue-eyed. But no one would accept such a description as correct in our times. This gradual disappearance of the light complexioned may be said, in one sense, to be due to a climate change that has been artificially produced. The starved, half-naked, and almost houseless peasant savage of the times of Cæsar struggled in his native forest with the cold. The well-fed, well-clothed, well-housed laborer now is literally living in a warmer and more genial climate. Glass windows that keep out the weather, wooden floors and stoves, have proved to be equivalent to a more southerly locality.

But it is not alone complexion that is altered; the form of the skull is also changed. We should here remember the well-ascertained fact that the skull is modeled by the brain, and not the brain compressed into form by the skull.

There are two typical forms of skull, popularly distinguished as the savage and the civilized. The former gives a detestable aspect to the countenance—a receding forehead, over which the hair encroaches on the eyebrows; the nostrils gaping, and seeming to enter directly backward into the head; the jaw projecting, the mouth open, the teeth uncovered. In the other the forehead is vertical; the brow expansive, and with an air of intellectuality; the face capable of expressing the most refined emotions; the eyes in an indescribable but significant manner manifest the exalted powers of the mind, and the lips are composed or compressed.

Between these two typical extremes there are many intermediate forms. Extreme heat or extreme cold, a life of physical hardship, tend to the production of the baser; a life of ease in a genial climate, to the higher type. And since our pursuits, and therefore our modes of thought, and therefore our feelings, depend upon the climate we are living in, its influences will be indicated by the general construction of the brain, and therefore by the form of the skull.

For perfection in the construction of the brain many conditions must be satisfied. It is not mere mass alone that is required, but also symmetrical organization of the several parts. The most prominent characteristic of this organ is its symmetrical doubleness. It consists of two halves, a right and a left; halves they ought hardly to be called, for each is complete in itself, and resembles its fellow. Every person has thus two perfect brains, each of which can conduct most of the usual mental acts. And, indeed, this symmetrical doubleness occurs throughout all that portion of the nervous system which is devoted, as physiologists term it, to animal life: so much so, that it might be affirmed that every person is composed of two symmetrical individuals, a right one and a left, which to a certain extent lead independent lives: for instance, one may be struck by palsy, the other may escape.

These double organs do not double the intensity of our perceptions, but only render them more precise. For current uses one side of the brain alone may be employed, but when we require greater exactness both are brought into play. They can give a separate, or a conjoint, or, as some singular facts show, an alternating action. How often, when one hemisphere is engaged in some ordinary pursuit requiring its steady application, does the other disturb it with suggestions of a different kind, as by a strain of music or by a line of poetry. We may indulge simultaneously in two trains of thought, but never in three, for the simple reason that we have a double, but not a triple brain. So, in the pleasing operation of castle-building, one hemisphere listens to the romance suggestions of the other, accepting them with gravity as if they were true, though very well knowing that its comrade is only telling it a lie.

Whatever interferes with the absolute equality of the right and left portions of the brain, affects the working of the mind. A skillful performer on the piano must use both hands with equal ease, and in like manner there is an ambi-dexterity of the brain. The metaphorical expression, a well-balanced mind, has really a profound scientific meaning. But, for securing in such a delicate organ as this absolute symmetry, how favorable all the external circumstances must be! An intolerable heat, a rigorous cold, misery, want, a depressed social state, render it almost impossible.

Such are some of the singular results of the separate operation of the two portions of the brain. In their conjoint action they present many facts well worthy of our attention. If one is inferior in organization to the other, it will, under certain circumstances, act discordantly, and insubordination or a want of consentaneous action occur. In many cases of insanity the healthy half is unable to control the diseased one, and hence we often observe in the insane that they have synchronously, or, at all events, in very rapid succession, two distinct trains of thought, and, consequently, two distinct utterances, each of which may be perfectly continuous, or even sane by itself, but the incongruities arising from the commingling of the two betray the condition of such persons. To a less marked extent—the same principle still, however, holding good—we may attribute the various declining degrees of mental brightness, until we come to persons who are intellectually quite obtuse and hardly able to reason. Such dullness may arise from a want of lateral symmetry, or from defective development of the organ as respects the three lobes it exhibits when viewed in the front and back direction, or from absolute deficiency in its size. In the former case, the overcoming of insubordination of one of the hemispheres may to a considerable extent be accomplished by education, of which one of the chief results is, that it exercises us in the habit of thinking of one thing at a time—of thinking, therefore, without confusion, and of arriving at conclusions with precision and decision.

But education, no matter how excellent it may be,

can never establish an intellectual equality among men. It can do no more than bring each up to the standard that the perfection of his brain admits. There it must stop; and hence in all communities there must be descending grades of humanity. The lower social strata have a different direction of thought from the higher. It is impossible to educate them completely, though it is possible to finish their education. It matters not in what direction their thoughts may be turned, the tokens of incapacity appear. Their conceptions of political progress dwindle into a change of men. In the face of endless disappointments, they think that they can gain their object by that inadequate device.

Now not unintentionally have I been led into this digression on the modes of action of the brain. That organ is the instrument through which the mind works. An artisan can never display his skill if his tools be imperfect; the mind can never demonstrate its innate excellence through a faulty apparatus. And hence we see that all that has been said about the influence of climate in controlling the development of man bears powerfully on this point. Our pursuits, our feelings, our modes of thought, depend on the theatre in which we live.

When a nation emigrates to a new country, the climate of which differs from that of the country it has left, it slowly passes through modifications, attempting, as it were, to adapt itself to the changed circumstances under which it has now to live. Many generations may be consumed before a complete correspondence between its physiological condition and the climate to which it is exposed is attained.

Its different classes will not make this movement with equal facility; some will accomplish it more quickly, others more slowly. Even when an equilibrium has been reached as completely as possible, there will still be distinct orders plainly enough perceptible among them. These orders depend upon a difference in individual intellectual development.

To bring these general principles to bear on the special case of the inhabitants of the United States, it is necessary to examine the topographical construction of the country, to examine its physical condition, its climate, its products, for such are the influences that model the character and determine the thoughts of men.

The United States reach from the Atlantic to the Pacific, from the Lakes to the Gulf of Mexico. The midst of this vast territory is depressed so as to form a valley, ranging north and south, drained by a noble river. The Missouri-Mississippi, arising from the convergence of hundreds of streams, is nearly 4500 miles long, and navigable for nearly 3800 miles.

This valley enjoys all the varieties of climate and all the diversities of physical character. At its limit in the far north it presents the vegetation of an almost sub-arctic country; at the south, opening into the Gulf of Mexico, it has all the luxuriant foliage of the tropics. Its upper end is flanked by the great lakes. They contain nearly twelve thousand cubic miles of water—it is said, though perhaps erroneously, half the fresh water of the globe! The gigantic character of the forms into which the continent is cast is illustrated by the Cataract of Niagara, the most imposing waterfall in the world.

On the east, the great valley is walled in by the ridge groups of the Alleghany system. At their foot is the Atlantic plain, reaching to the Atlantic Ocean, nearly level, and raised but little above that sea. This plain increases from a few miles in width at the north, to 150 at the south. It is intersected by a ridge of primary rocks, over which its rivers fall, and which in many places is the tide boundary and head of navigation. This ledge therefore determines the sites of many of the large towns or centres of commerce. The plain itself is full of swamps, morasses, sluggish streams. It is infested with fever.

On the west, leaving the line of the Mississippi and ascending the incline that culminates in the Pacific coast mountains, the aspect of Nature exhibits a gradual change. At first, in the ravines, there are thickets of the long-leaved willow, and roses, the most beautiful of the prairie flowers. Antelopes and

Deer run over the hills. In every direction the leaves of the prairie sage shine like silver as the wind turns them up to the sun. The streams are fringed with cottonwood and groves of oak, tenanted by flocks of turkeys. As the traveler advances, the cacti—plants that love dryness—become more and more numerous, and the shifting sands are worked into hills by the wind. In the streams, the beaver, yearly diminishing in numbers, builds his dam; on the plains the prairie dog excavates his subterraneous village.

Still more westwardly, the characteristic of the country is its extreme dryness. In a long day's journey water may not be met with. As the elevation increases, every thing looks as if it had been swept by fire; even the stunted and dead pines present the prevailing dull, ash-colored hue of desolation. The bare hills assume grotesque forms of domes and minarets, half deceiving the traveler into the belief that he is approaching some city of magicians in the desert. In this sandy and sterile region, the rich herbage and nutritious grasses, that had furnished on the immense prairies pasturage for countless thousands of buffaloes, have given place to odoriferous plants with shrunken leaves. The snow line of the mountains, which even in the height of summer whitens the horizon, marks out the culminating ridge. The topography of the West differs from that of the East in this, that the highest range of mountains is nearest to the sea. The Coast Range and the Sierra Nevada surpass the Rocky Mountains. The Columbia River alone breaks through the enormous barrier, and, in a region of gigantic pines, delivers its waters into the Pacific Ocean.

Such is the domain of the United States. It is necessary, next, to consider its climate. On climate depends the distribution of vegetable and animal life; it also determines the pursuits and character of men.

If a traveler leaves the coast of New England and goes to the West, he encounters successively four well-marked strands of climate. On the sea-board the temperature is moderated by the ocean; at a little distance in the interior there is an excessive contrast in the seasons; gaining the region of the lakes, a moderate climate is again met with, and still beyond that another excessive one. These vicissitudes arise from the action of great bodies of water, such as the Atlantic and the Lakes, in equalizing the heat. Along those parallels of latitude the mean annual temperature varies very little. The climate difference is due to the unequal distribution of heat among the seasons.

In excessive climates winter abruptly changes into summer with scarcely any intervening spring, and vegetation receives a sudden impulse. The character of man is also affected; for its proper development a succession of seasons is necessary. The absence of summer is the absence of taste and genius; where there is no winter loyalty is unknown.

From the North let us turn to the South. If a traveler leaves the Atlantic coast of Upper Florida, where a high temperature always predominates, the Ocean and the Mexican Gulf conjointly control the heat, and the seasons glide into one another without marked extremes. There is a perpetual verdure. The Palmetto, the Orange, the Fig, grow without danger from the frost. There is no longer that violent contrast between summer and winter experienced at the North. For instance, at Fort Snelling, in Minn., the difference of the mean temperature of those seasons is 56°; in Florida it is scarcely 12°. The skies are also clearer. While on the Lakes there are only 117 fair days in a year, on the Florida coast there are more than 250.

Though it is only a mere fringe of country that I have here considered, enough has been said to bring into relief the chief conclusion at which those who have carefully and attentively studied this subject have long ago arrived, viz., that the climate is more equable in the South than it is in the North. The irresistible consequence of this is, that in the South the pursuits of men have a greater sameness, their interests are more identical, they think and act alike.

In the North, the avocations of men must exhibit great differences. On the sea-board the commercial and manufacturing element must predominate; then, through a broad zone, the agricultural. Ascending the incline to the mountain range, they must become mineralogical, a similar variation occurring in an inverse order as the descent is made to the Pacific. The sandy desert can not fail to impress its special effects. These variations of interests and pursuits must produce a more heterogeneous population, and a great difference in intentions and thoughts.

Let us look at this more closely. Let us recall some of those results which Physiologists and Philosophical historians have proved to be the consequences of those influences in Europe—results none the less interesting because they are old. Though holding good for another continent, they suggest applications in ours.

In the North the alternation of winter and summer allots for the life of man distinct and different duties. Summer is the season of outdoor labor, winter is spent in the dwelling. In the South labor may be continuous, though it may vary. The Northern man must do to-day that which the Southern man may put off till to-morrow. For this reason the Northern man must be industrious; the Southern may be indolent, having less foresight and a less tendency to regulated habits. The cold, bringing with it a partial cessation from labor, affords also an opportunity for forethought and reflection; and hence the Northern man acquires a habit of not acting without consideration, and is slower in the initiation of his movements. The Southern man is prone to act without reflection; he does not fairly weigh the last consequences of what he is about to do. The one is cautious, the other impulsive. Winter, with its cheerlessness and discomforts, gives to the Northern man his richest blessing; it teaches him to cling to his hearthstone and his family. In times of war that blessing proves to be his weakness; he is vanquished if his dwelling be seized. The Southern man cares nothing for that. Cut off from the promptings of external Nature for so large a portion of the year, the mind in the North becomes self-occupied; it contents itself with but few ideas, which it considers from many points of view. It is apt to fasten itself intently on one, and pursue it with fanatical perseverance. A Southern nation, which is continually under the influence of the sky, which is continually prompted to varying thoughts, will indulge in a superfluity of ideas, and deal with them all superficially; more volatile than reflective, it can never have a constant love for a fixed constitution. Once resolved to act, the intention of the North, sustained by reason alone, will outlast the enthusiasm of the South. In physical courage the two are equal; but the

North will prevail, through its habits of labor, of method, and its inexorable perseverance. Long ago, writers who have paid attention to these subjects have affirmed that the South will fight for the benefit of its leaders, but the North will conquer for the benefit of all. To convince the man who lives under a roof, an appeal must be made to his understanding; to convince him who lives under the sky, the appeal must be to his feelings.

Such are some of the general consequences ensuing from the action of climate upon men, and such represent the effects which are occurring or have occurred on the population of the North American continent. The description I have given of this vast theatre of human life, though very superficial, is yet sufficient to impress the reader with a conviction of the wonderful variations of climate it presents—great differences in annual mean temperature, and still greater ones in the distribution of heat through the seasons.

But heat is only one of the controlling vital conditions. There are equally striking contrasts in the moisture and dryness of different regions; in the number of fair and of rainy days in the year; in the range of movement in the barometer—that is, in the pressure of the air; in the brightness of the light, or in its reverse dullness or cloudiness of the skies; in topographical altitudes above the level of the sea. These and very many more such physical influences exhibit a surprising complexity; and yet the more insignificant, as well as the more important, impress modifications on the constitution of man.

From this, therefore, it follows that such a continent, when its inhabitants shall have reached a concordance with the conditions to which they are exposed, will present numberless examples of modified men; the type from which they originated yielding helplessly to the powers operating upon it, and suffering variations not only in complexion, but in interior constitution too. And since the American continent not only rivals, but exceeds the continent of Europe in these differences, it necessarily follows that the families of modified men destined eventually to be found upon it will be correspondingly more numerous than those now found on the Continent of Europe. The great differences so strikingly observed in the intellectual conceptions, and even in the manner of thinking, in the Old World, will be exceeded in the New.

That social stagnation so characteristic of Asia depends primarily on the equilibrium that has been attained, in the lapse of many ages, between the strands of its population and the climate zones in which they dwell. To no insignificant extent may the same be perceived in Europe, especially among the lower, that is, among the less locomotive portion of the inhabitants. But in no part of America has that exact concordance as yet had time or opportunity to be truly established, though in the Southern States an approach has been made to it. Moreover, the climate is continually undergoing local modifications through the operations of agriculture and other causes, and the conditions under which life is carried on in civilized communities are varying through the introduction of new and important inventions. The construction of houses, and the means of combating the rigors of winter by the better warming of them; the increasing resort to a preservation of ice, to meet in various applications the heats of summer; a habit of resorting to higher and cooler regions for the same purpose, are all having their effect. And, what is of not less importance, the daily food of extensive districts is changing. Improved means of locomotion are bringing within the reach of the consumer, even though he may be in the less affluent station of life, articles to which he was formerly a stranger.

Those improved means of locomotion likewise stimulate all classes to travel. In America a journey of a thousand miles is considered, even by the laboring population, as a small affair scarce needing any preparation. The necessary result of such personal mobility is, that families are perpetually changing their places of abode. The physiological equilibrium which might have been attained by a more stationary life is procrastinated. Society presents the aspect of an ever-changing, ever-struggling mass—a state of things the very opposite to that observed in Asia.

Uniformity of climate makes people homogeneous. They will necessarily think alike, and inevitably act alike.

Where variation in successive generations is not taking place, immobility in national institutions is possible.

The first and most important condition for the prosperity of a great nation is stability in its institutions.

But stability must be carefully distinguished from immobility. We must bear in mind that the affairs of men are ever changing; successive generations live under essentially different conditions; public necessities are therefore continually varying, and disorder arises as soon as Institutions prescribe one course and Necessity demands another.

To insure stability, the political system must therefore admit of change—that change being in accordance with a law of variation which depends on a fixed principle. Unchangeability should belong to the law, not to the institutions issuing from it.

In that manner alone can order and progress coexist, and the demand made by modern statesmanship with so much solicitude be satisfied. It truly affirms that there can be no real Order without Progress, and no real Progress without Order.

Institutions well adapted for five millions of people will certainly be very unsuitable for fifty. Institutions intended for a narrow coast line will certainly be inadequate if applied to one of the quarters of the globe. Edifices, though they may be built of iron, will fall to pieces if the architect has not made provision for expansion at one point and contraction at another. Where motion must in the necessities of the case occur, it is essential for safety that there should be a harmony among the moving parts. Inequality of progressive movement implies strain—strain implies fracture.

It is therefore the province of statesmanship to determine how change shall be provided for in political institutions, and what is the true nature of the law by which they shall be modified. Above all, it is its province to discover the immutable principles on which that law must rest.

It is better for communities to advance through legal forms than by revolutionary impulses, or by attempting to secure stability through incessantly failing experiments. The only safe guide for them to follow is furnished by a careful investigation of the circumstances under which their life has been and is to be spent.

The life of a feeble colony is simple. When it has become a widespread and powerful nation, its necessities are numerous and contradictory. The chances that they will be contradictory increase as the physical circumstances of the country are more diversified.

Hence it is that a nation lying east and west will generally have less discordant interests than one the range of which is north and south. Climate varies in this latter case much more than it does in the former.

Society, therefore, pressed upon relentlessly by Nature, passes through a definite series of changes. It runs through a predestined career. It is never in a state of rest, as politicians too often suppose, but always in motion. It has a past from which it is coming, a future to which it is going. It also has an unavoidable end.

A nation, as it passes from phase to phase, is guided by definite natural laws, and depends upon definite conditions. There must be an unfailing supply of new parts to take the place of the old that are being unceasingly removed. There must also be a simultaneous grouping or moulding. Its life is to outlast by far the life of any of its constituent parts, or even of many generations of them. Its wants and its wishes will vary with circumstances and times. Half-educated people vainly persuade themselves, and demagogues try to persuade others, that it is possible to devise a political constitution so perfect that it will never need change. A constitution may be intrinsically good in so far as it suits a present generation and a short time. But there is goodness of a higher order, depending on a plasticity that can adapt itself to varying circumstances and stand the shocks of Time.

In the popular view, a nation arises independently of others. Without any disturbance it might never have existed. But nations should not be regarded as isolated forms. They are, in reality, an organic series connected together. Each has bonds with those that are past and with those that are to come. In its position each is perfect in itself. It is an incarnation of natural influences upon humanity at a given epoch. There is, therefore, a chain of Empires, whose first link is far back in the darkness of pre-historic times.

Such an interconnected succession implies cause and effect—the steady dominion of natural law. It means the continuous advancement of humanity.

From infancy man slowly emerges into childhood, from that into youth, from that to maturity. Each of these stages brings with it changes of character, making him feel differently and think differently. In that resistless development have we any voluntary concern? Could we have arrested its march by any desire, or could we have diverted its course? We have made the same passage that has fallen to the lot of every human being, and as for our predecessors, so for us, there awaits us the unpitying grave. We came into the world without our own knowledge, we are departing from it against our own will.

In that great branch of literature of which we now only see the dim beginning—Comparative History—the series of Nations, viewed by the light of individual life, will be hereafter considered. Nations will be regarded not as mere accidents, or creative blunders, or experimental attempts, but as emerging from the bosom of humanity through predetermining causes. It will treat of their march of development, showing why one has been arrested at an early stage in its life, another has advanced more completely to maturity, another has expended its vital powers, and died, as it were, of old age. It will show that there is a general equation of National life, and that special nations are special solutions of it. It will prove that nations are not individuals, but only forms into which humanity is thrown—mere transitory combinations, of which the inevitable issue is dissolution, death. For the constituent men of whom they were composed there may be an immortality, but that does not imply immortality for the resulting form. The material particles of which the flame of a lamp is composed we know are indestructible, eternal, but who shall say whither that flame has gone when once blown out!

Perhaps I can not more impressively enforce the principles that have been explained on the foregoing pages, particularly those that assert the control of Climate over the actions of man, than by presenting one or two historical reminiscences. From many instances, I select the cases of Egypt and of Asia.

European civilization originated in Egypt. For thirty-four centuries before our era that country was governed by dynasties of kings succeeding each other without interruption. Its soil, proverbially fertile, sustained a population estimated in the most prosperous times at about seven millions; and repeated military expeditions into Asia and Ethiopia had, in the course of ages, concentrated in it immense wealth, and crowded with captives and slaves the valley of the Nile.

Until about seven hundred years before Christ the inhabitants of that country had been shut out from all Mediterranean or European contact by a rigorous exclusion exceeding that until recently practiced in China and Japan. As from the inmates of "The Happy Valley" in Rasselas no tidings escaped into the outer world, so to the European the Valley of the Nile was a region of mysteries and marvels. Uncertain legends were current all over Asia Minor, Greece, Italy, Sicily, of the prodigies and miracles that adventurous pirates reported they had actually seen in their stealthy visits to the enchanted valley—great pyramids covering acres of land, their tops rising to the heavens, yet each pyramid nothing more than the tombstone of a king—Colossi sitting on granite thrones, the images of Pharaohs who had lived in the morning of the world, still silently looking upon the land which thousands of years before they had ruled; of these, some, obedient to the Sun, saluted his approach when touched by his morning rays — Obelisks of prodigious height, carved by superhuman skill from a single block of stone, and raised by superhuman power erect on their everlasting pedestals, their faces covered with mysterious hieroglyphics, a language unknown to the vulgar, telling by whom and for what they had been constructed — Temples, the massive leaning and lowering walls of which were supported by countless ranges of statues—avenues of Sphinxes, through the shadows of which, grim and silent, the portals of fanes might be approached — Catacombs containing the mortal remains of many generations, each corpse awaiting in mysterious embalmment a future life—Labyrinths of many hundred chambers and vaults, into which whoso entered without a clew never again escaped, but in the sameness and silence of those endless windings found his sepulchre.

In the security of this inaccessible retreat, and under political institutions of a favorable character, the civilization which was to be conferred, through

Greece on Europe originated. Each year since the country has been open to investigation and its hieroglyphic system understood, the impressions we receive of its intellectual advancement have been more and more favorable. The vocal statue of Memnon at Thebes, it is said, emitted a musical sound when touched by the rays of the sun. In the light of modern criticism, every obelisk and monument of those desolated palaces is finding a voice.

As a critical attention is bestowed by modern scholars upon Egyptian remains, we learn more truly what is the place in history of that venerable country. From Egypt, it now appears, were derived the prototypes of the Greek architectural orders, and even their ornaments and conventional designs; thence came the models of the Greek and Etruscan vases; thence many of the ante-Homeric legends—the accusation of the dead, the trial before the judges of Hell, the reward and punishment of every man, the dog Cerberus, the Stygian stream, the lake of oblivion, the piece of money, Charon and his boat, the fields of Elysium, the islands of the blessed. Thence came the first ritual for the dead, litanies to the Sun, and painted or illuminated missals; thence came the dogma of a queen of heaven. What other country ever offered such noble and enduring edifices to the gods?—temples with avenues of sphinxes—massive pylons adorned with obelisks in front, which even imperial Rome and modern Paris have not thought it beneath them to appropriate—porticoes and halls of columns on which were carved the portraits of kings and the effigies of gods. The Pyramids have seen the Old Empire, the Hyksos monarchs, the New Empire, the Persian, the Macedonian, the Roman, the Mohammedan. They have stood still, while heaven itself has changed. They were already five hundred years old when the Southern Cross disappeared from the horizon of the countries of the Baltic. The Pole Star itself is a new comer to them. Another and a more brilliant star, now far removed, then occupied that conspicuous place.

What was it that thus placed Egypt in the van of our civilization, and gave her the precedence of Europe?

The progress of human generations is shaped by the physical circumstances in which they live.

The Nile, the mysterious river of antiquity—mysterious now no more—takes a northerly direction from equatorial Africa through a valley, overflowing its banks once each year, spreading a fertile mud to the edge of the sandy desert, and encroaching perpetually on the Mediterranean Sea. All Lower Egypt has been made by it. The arable strand thus formed varies in width from two to about eleven miles.

In one all-important particular Egypt differed from most other places—the agricultural result of its sea sons could be foretold. Elsewhere men depend for the fruits of the earth on uncertain rains, in Egypt they depended on the inundations. If in the month of July the water has only risen twelve feet, it is known that the harvests will be scanty; if to twenty-one feet, that they will be plentiful. A system of reservoirs and dikes, floodgates and other hydraulic apparatus, had been contrived in the remotest times. The government took charge of the river, delivering water from it in a regulated manner, and remunerating itself by a tax.

Agriculture thus became a reliable art. The people were relieved from the uncertainties of the future. The river was to them all a common interest, a common bond of union. Where there is a bond like that, its political consequences can hardly be exaggerated. Moreover, the climate throughout the whole of Egypt proper was very uniform.

The remark has already been made on a previous page that uniformity of Climate makes people homogeneous. They will necessarily think alike, and inevitably act alike.

Here, then, was a people having common ideas and common intentions. Its consolidation and civilization were assured. A Colossus with its hands resting upon its knees typified what the nation really was. Every thing seemed eternal, no change probable, no catastrophe possible.

It is not surprising, then, that the two great divisions of the country—Upper and Lower Egypt—became consolidated at an early epoch, and in all the vicissitudes of prosperity and adversity were never subsequently separated.

In this invariable climate, held together by a common interest and a common bond, generations of Egyptians for forty centuries and more succeeded one another. Each one was like all its predecessors. There was nothing to produce modification. The mould into which Nature poured her living material underwent no kind of change. The casts that she procured were all alike.

Egypt is therefore an exemplification of the general principle that where variation in successive generations is not taking place, immobility in national institutions is possible.

Of Asia it has long been remarked that it is a continent without any temperate zone. The vast mountain axis which in an irregular manner divides it, throws it into two slopes, one looking to the north, the other to the south. Apart, however, from this, which undoubtedly impresses a general feature of violent contrast on its meteorology, its local variations are such as to give rise to many diversities of climate, marked in a sufficiently distinct manner, though not so abrupt or so frequent as is the case in Europe. It necessarily, therefore, presents numerous examples of distinctly modified men.

Receiving its human population at an epoch anterior to that of the peopling of Europe, Asia has always been regarded as the birthplace of man. On a previous page has been given a portion of that large body of evidence accumulated by Comparative Philologists in proof of the fact that the present inhabitants of Europe are of Oriental descent.

The activity that must have existed in its early history, when from one, or at the most a few centres, its teeming population was rapidly spreading in every direction, and accomplishing the settlement of its various districts, has long ago given place to stagnation. At intervals centuries apart there have poured from it devastating hordes that have precipitated themselves on Europe. These have commonly melted away in the populations they overran, and have scarcely left any trace of their existence in the countries from which they emerged.

In some instances such warlike emigrating columns have been set in motion by military chieftains or by internal civil commotions; but not unfrequently they have originated, there is every reason to believe, in the consequences of those geological changes to which the Eastern Continent is subject—changes which divert the courses of rivers and modify the lines of travel. On the nomadic population of the northern slope such effects are widespread disasters, compelling the tribes into a forced emigration down the gentle incline—the path zone—that leads out of Asia into Europe.

Exception made of these convulsive social movements, the entire population of that continent is in a stagnant condition. There is nothing to excite locomotion. At the best, the numberless states and forms of government existing, restrict intercommunication within very narrow bounds. Over vast tracts of country the traveler can not pass without risk of liberty or life. So many different languages, so many different chieftains, present insuperable obstacles to movement.

The influence of religious opinions also exerts a powerful effect. Among many millions it is thought unholy to go to sea. The lines of journey, such as they are, remain unaltered and unimproved for successive centuries—unaltered unless by the movements or acts of Nature. The venerable caravanserai receives its evening travelers just as it did centuries ago. The patient camel on the southwestern slope, and the rude wagon on the northern, pursue their wearisome courses just as they did in the days of Alexander.

It may therefore be said that the Asiatic populations have truly lost locomotion — they have become stationary, vast multitudes during their whole lives scarcely leaving the places where they were born. Successive ages have left an indelible impression. In all directions, the people have come into physiological correspondence with the natural conditions in which they are living. In this perfect correspondence lies the secret of their stagnant state.

Stagnant it emphatically is! There are no changes in the fashions of clothing, no improvements in the habitations, no bettering of food. As their ancestors in past times lived, so do they. Oppression may have sometimes driven them to revolt, the intrigues of leading men may have sometimes plunged them into war, but it never occurs to them to modify the political system under which they may happen to live, any more than it occurs to bees to change the economy of their hive. The utmost they ever accomplish is to exchange their tyrant. They do not seek to get rid of the tyranny. In Asia the sense of political improvement is lost. Crushed by the relentless tread of centuries, they can only appreciate tranquillity and rest. Without a murmur or even a wish, they leave Europe to seek and sigh for freedom.

To this correspondence which the lapse of time has accomplished between their physiological condition and the theatre of their life, we must attribute that propensity to religious aspirations which has for so long marked their character, and which has so profoundly impressed all other portions of the world.

Buddhism, Mohammedanism, Judaism, the religious faiths of nearly eight hundred millions of men, are all of Asiatic origin. Moreover, it must not be forgotten that Palestine was the birthplace of Christianity. The irrepressible tendency of Europe is to philosophy, that of Asia is to religion. The former looks forth on the exterior world, investigating the events of Nature, and profiting by the application of the discoveries it makes. The latter looks inwardly upon itself. Motionless, like its own Fakirs, it is absorbed in self-contemplation, and has fallen into a trance.

It was not, however, always thus in the East. In times of which History has failed to preserve any account, that continent must have been the scene of prodigious human activity. In it were first developed those fundamental inventions and discoveries which really lie at the basis of the progress of the human race—the subjugation of domestic animals, the management of fire, the expression of thought by writing. We are apt to overlook how much man must have done, how much he must have added to his natural powers in pre-historic times. We forget how many contributions to our own comforts are of Oriental origin. Their commonness hides them from our view. If the European wishes to know how much he owes to the Asiatic, he has only to cast a glance at an hour of his daily life. The clock which summons him from his bed in the morning was the invention of the East, as also were clepsydras and sun-dials. The prayer for his daily bread, that he has said from his infancy, first rose from the side of a Syrian mountain. The linens and cottons with which he clothes himself, though they may be very fine, are inferior to those that have been made for time immemorial in the looms of India. The silk was stolen by some missionaries for his benefit from China. He could buy better steel than that with which he shaves himself in the old city of Damascus, where it was first invented. The coffee he expects at breakfast was first grown by the Arabians, and the natives of Upper India prepared the sugar with which he sweetens it. A school-boy can tell the meaning of the Sanscrit words sacchara canda. If his tastes are light and he prefers tea, the virtues of that excellent leaf were first pointed out by the industrious Chinese. They also taught him how to make and use the cup and saucer in which to serve it. His breakfast tray was lacquered in Japan. There is a tradition that leavened bread was first made of the waters of the Ganges. The egg he is breaking was laid by a fowl whose ancestors were first domesticated by the Malaccans, unless she may have been—though that will not alter the case—a modern Shanghai. If there are preserves and fruits on his board, let him remember with thankfulness that Persia first gave him the Cherry, the Peach, the Plum. If in any of these pleasant preparations he detects the flavor of alcohol, let it remind him that that substance was first distilled by the Arabians, who have set him the praiseworthy example, which it will be for his benefit to follow, of abstaining from its use. When he talks about coffee and alcohol, he is using Arabic words. A thousand years before it had occurred to him to enact laws of restriction in the use of intoxicating drinks, the Prophet of Mecca did the same thing, and, what is more to the purpose, has compelled to this day all Asia and Africa to obey them. We gratify our taste for personal ornaments in the way the Orientals have taught us—with pearls, rubies, sapphires, diamonds. Of public amusements it is the same. The most magnificent fireworks are still to be seen in India and China; and as regards the pastimes of private life, Europe has produced no invention that can rival the game of Chess. We have no hydraulic constructions as great as the Chinese Canal, no fortifications as extensive as the Chinese Wall; we have no Artesian wells that can at all approach in depth some of theirs. We have not yet resorted to the practice of obtaining coal gas from the interior of the earth; they have borings for that purpose more than 3000 feet deep.

Through the long-continued influence of Climate action a different mental constitution has been imparted to the inhabitants of Europe and of Asia. The mind of the latter has become essentially synthetic, that of the former analytic. The Asiatic is the creator of systems of Theology, Law, Philosophy, some of which have endured for thousands of years, and have been adopted by a large portion of the human race. The European pursues his course in a way less grand, but which, since it has a better ascertained foundation, leads to more certain, and, as the course of centuries will show, more powerful, widespread, and equally lasting results. In Asia, as we have seen, customs and fashions remain invariable; every thing is in a state, as we term it, of stagnation, or, as they consider it, of repose. On the other hand, the analytical tendency of the European has led to the intellectual and political anarchy of our times, when fundamental doctrines of every kind are called in question, and scarcely two men can be found whose views on religious, political, and social questions coincide. In Asia there are no questions, only affirmations. Europe, except when the Church for a thousand years enforced the Asiatic system, has ever been prone to ask questions. Since the fourteenth century, when she returned to that propensity, she has been passing through a chaos of doubt in the innumerable answers she receives.

I trace, therefore, the stagnant condition of the Asiatic populations to that correspondence into which they have slowly been brought with the physical circumstances in which they live. They have come into a condition of physiological repose. The consequence is, that they have come into a condition of political repose also. Barriers not only of a material, but of an intellectual kind, the consequences of those events, are now fettering them, cramping them. They are held in the iron grasp of a hundred tyrannies, and, what is indeed more effectual, are parted from one another by many different tongues.

The consequence of this physiological correspondence has been the permanent establishment of the various governments that divide the continent. These may from time to time suffer interior change through civil commotions or mutual war, but the aspect of Oriental life has remained unaltered for several thousand years. The many National forms that have sprung into existence tend to aid Climate in its influence and perpetuate a common effect. From being originally consequences, they have assumed the attitude of causes.

And yet it is not beyond the bounds of possibility that this deplorable state of things should change, and, those old, worn-out populations disappearing, races of new-comers take their place—new-comers arising, perhaps, in large part from the intermixture of people who, not having that physiological correspondence with the countries in which they were thrown, could renew the scene of struggle, the scene of activity again. Asia has given to Europe its religion. Europe may hereafter repay the debt by giving to Asia her improved means of locomotion. Once let those torpid communities be set in movement, once mix them up again by travel, by commerce, and, by their consequence, intermarriage, and the aspect of things would quickly change. In Europe itself, the rapid modes of locomotion—inappreciably valuable inventions of our age—are inciting an impending revolution. They extend the sphere of individual life; bring diverse populations, that misinterpreted and misunderstood one another, face to face; remove national prejudices; refine the public manners; and elevate the public mind. Asia, the land of miracles, may yet be destined to exhibit the greatest of political wonders. Interior motion may revolutionize that continent.

Turning from these special cases, to which many others might be added if there were occasion, I shall now endeavor to bring plainly into relief the facts that have been considered in the preceding pages. What is it they amount to? This—that the body of man can not resist external influences. It is helplessly modified by heat and cold, dryness, moisture—that is, by Climate. The complexion of the skin changes, as also does the construction of the brain.

In a restricted locality there may therefore be a sameness in the population; but in a vast continent, where there are all kinds of climate, there will inevitably be all kinds of modified men. Their thoughts and their actions must necessarily be diverse. To unite them under one government becomes, then, proportionably more and more difficult. But now, if there be a point on which America as a nation has come to an irrevocable resolve, it is that one government alone shall hold sway on this continent. Then let us look the physical difficulty plainly in the face. Though formidable, it is not insuperable.

Look at that zone of American population inhabiting the countries in which the cotton-plant can grow. Does not the luxuriance of that delicate product, that so quickly suffers on the approach of cold, imply a homogeneous climate? Is it surprising that there should be a mental sameness, a concordance among the inhabitants in their manner of thinking? We have seen that a common climate makes men think alike and act alike.

Turn now to that other zone, stretching from the Atlantic westwardly in the direction of the great lakes. Here there is none of that climate homogeneousness occurring in the other case. Even before the region of the lakes is fairly reached, four distinct strands of different temperature have been passed through. Follow that zone with a prophetic eye, as it becomes peopled to the shores of the Pacific Ocean, and tell me, as those busy hordes extend over the vast sandy desert, climb up the threatening ridges of the mountain chains, descend through the moaning forests of enormous pines beyond, how many are the vicissitudes through which life must be maintained, and I will tell you how many distinct families of men there must be.

We must steadily bear in mind the principle that has forced itself so strongly on our attention. Scientific Physiology has no better ascertained fact than that man possesses no innate resistance to change. The moment he leaves his accustomed place of abode to encounter new physical conditions and altered modes of life, that moment his structure commences slowly to change. It may take several generations before an equilibrium is reached. Then his countenance, his complexion, his hair, testify to what has been going on.

Public policy should therefore hold these great facts steadily in view, and shape its course accordingly. It should not only discern herein the hidden causes of those dreadful events through which, as a Nation, we are passing, it should also foresee that this is the rugged path through which, in the future, destiny leads us. To the innate sympathies and antipathies thus engendered the demagogue will in all future time appeal. As they have done in our day, so will they ever hereafter constitute an instrument apt for his purpose. We have been called upon to deal with the variations as they now exist, our descendants will have to deal with the greater variations coming. No European nation can serve us as an exemplar, for none has encountered a problem so complicated and vast. The nearest approach to its solution was made by the Roman Empire, but that lay, for the most part, in an easterly and westerly direction, in which the wants and intentions of men were very much the same. That imperial system was intrinsically unable to extend itself north and south. Had it made such an extension, the difficulty of its government would have been far greater than it was. Whoever will study its disintegration and disruption will see how true these principles are.

And here I can not help making the remark, that whoever accepts these principles as true, and bears in mind how physical circumstances control the deeds of men, as it may be said, in spite of themselves, will have a disposition to look with generosity on the acts of political enemies. Even when in madness they have rushed to the dread arbitrament of civil war—a crime in the face of which all other crimes are as nothing—and brought upon their country immeasurable woes, he will distinguish the instrument from the cause, and, when he has overpowered, will forgive.

Philosophy alone can raise man to that grand elevation which enables him to perform acts that centuries will admire. Philosophy alone can place him

> "Above all pain, all passion, and all pride,
> Above the reach of flattery's baleful breath,
> The lust of lucre, and the dread of death."

There are things that no human legislation can accomplish. Perhaps he who considers the supreme difficulties incident to our political position may look at the picture almost in despair, and come to the conclusion that in such a case no human statesmanship can avail.

But let us take courage. Once in the history of the world has a parallel attempt at the union of a continent been made. In the eleventh century was born a great man, who resolved to convert all Europe into one federation, with the Sovereign Pontiff at its head, and Emperors and Kings his proconsuls —that Europe which, as we have seen, presents all sorts of climates and all kinds of modified men. A religious foundation was, under the circumstances, the only one that could be given to the contemplated structure; but Gregory VII. saw not only its capabilities, but its defects, as any one may find who will consider his relations with the heretic Berengar. Those defects he would have remedied if he could, and brought that foundation into more complete accordance with human reason.

What was the practical instrument on which Gregory VII. relied in carrying out his intention? His legates could pass from Scotland to Spain, from the Atlantic to the confines of Asia, and meet in every monastery and at every church men speaking the same tongue. The Latin language gave him intelligent allies all over Christendom, but allies only among the men of education. With us, how much better is the prospect—one language from ocean to ocean, and that among the lowly as well as the high. That bond of union is for us a bond of strength. It aids in compensating for diversities of climate. It gives us a common history of the past, a common hope for the future. Conterminous groups of men are far more effectually isolated by different forms of speech than by intervening rivers and mountains, but groups that are far apart may be in communion through a common tongue. They may learn to have faith in the greatness and permanence of their political creations, and in unbroken unity discern unconquerable power.

With such an inappreciable advantage in our favor, we are encouraged to look again at the great problem before us, and to ask, Can we not neutralize those climate differences, which, if unchecked, must transmute us into different nations?

In two words, I think, we find an answer—Education and Intercommunication. Nor is this the suggestion of mere theorists. Under that formula four hundred millions of men—one third of the human race—have found stability for their institutions in China. By their public school system they have organized their national intellect; by their canal system they have made themselves, though living in a climate as diversified as ours, essentially one people. The principle on which their political system is thus founded has for many thousand years confronted successfully all human variations, and has outlived all revolutions. But what is their public education compared with what ours might be? what is their canal system compared with what our railroads will become?

Of education I shall have nothing more to say, for all intelligent persons concur in the belief that it is absolutely necessary to the perpetuity of the American system. The public value of locomotion is by no means so well understood. While legislation has in all directions been brought to bear on the protection, encouragement, development of the former; the latter, it may be said, has been altogether neglected in a national point of view.

Talleyrand, when speaking of the United States to the Emperor Napoleon, made this remark: "It is a giant without bones." That was before there were any railroads; but since his day the bones have begun to grow, and they are bones of iron.

Now, since there is an unceasing tendency to the modification of the human system by the operation of climate, and evils ensue both by a community coming into repose, which is politically falling into a stagnant condition, and by the antagonisms that arise between conterminous communities that have thus passed into different states, it is very plain that the thing of primary importance to be accomplished is, as far as may be possible, to prevent such climate actions reaching their full effect. This can only be done by promoting locomotion.

It is therefore unwise to give legislative encouragement to any thing that may tend to make communities, or even families, too stationary. Fortunately, the intentions of the statesman, in this respect, are greatly facilitated by the established usages respecting the inheritance of property and the incessant breaking up of estates. Not less effectual is the system of agriculture, if such it can be called, that we pursue—our practice of killing land. A soil that has undergone exhaustion of certain of its essential ingredients, as bone-earth, potash, or the like, can not be economically restored. It is much cheaper to abandon the ruined estate and move to the virgin lands of the West. That love of the homestead, so characteristic of the settled populations of Europe, can scarcely be said to exist among us. The children leave their father's hearth without reluctance, for he is perpetually anticipating leaving it himself. It might have been feared—perhaps was feared by many observant persons—that this loss of local patriotism would imply the loss of national sentiment, but the experience of the civil war has shown the incorrectness of such a foreboding. The history of the world can not furnish a more splendid example of unwavering fortitude, unshrinking self-sacrifice, in vindication of national life. The acts of which it has been our privilege to be eye-witnesses, will by future generations of Americans be pointed to with pride as the greatest glory of their history—an incentive in their inevitable march to imperial greatness, a firm support in their days of trial.

The customs and usages of American domestic life have therefore, to a certain extent, made us a locomotive people. Not without reason have many foreign travelers affirmed that we are essentially a nomadic race. It is well for our future that we are so.

It should be a settled principle of American legislation to encourage in every possible manner facilities for intercommunication, to repress in the most effectual way any thing that might possibly act as a restraint.

From the results of the policy that has been pursued in the case of the Post-office system, very valuable suggestions may be gathered. By reducing the cost of the transmission of letters and newspapers to the smallest possible amount, conspicuous social advantages have been gained. The family tie has been knit in spite of separation, the public intellect has been enlarged by the diffusion of general information. That mental activity which arises from the concentration of masses of men in great cities is felt sympathetically in the most sparsely peopled and distant country places. During the civil war metropolitan journalism has every where been recognized as a living power.

But it is not enough that there should be free movement for thought; free movement for the people themselves is of equal importance. That is the true method for combating climate effects—preventing communities from falling into Asiatic torpor, and contracting senseless antipathies against each other. Had the Southern States for the last ten years been pervaded by an unceasing stream of Northern travel in every direction, the civil war would not have occurred.

Experience shows that travel increases as its cost diminishes. Whatever, therefore, operates as a tax on locomotion, is inconsistent with the highest principles of state policy. No community should be permitted to take advantage of the geographical position it may happen to occupy for the purpose of exacting a toll for its own profit. Such practices may suit an Arab sheikh or other Asiatic chieftain, who levies a contribution on the passing caravan, but is altogether inadmissible in a modernized society. A community can not perpetrate this act without becoming politically debauched and demoralized. It is an offense against the highest public interests.

When the Railway system was first being developed in England, measures were taken to give to the government an eventual and thorough control over it. Already in that country it is agitated to consummate those measures by the State assuming the proprietorship of the roads, equalizing their rates of charge, and reducing those rates to a minimum. There can be no doubt that such a consummation would produce very powerful social effects. In its direction it would act in the same manner that the changes in the postal system have done, those social effects being all of an advantageous kind. But England, her comparatively restricted geographical extent being considered, is not pressed by those climate considerations that are of such paramount importance in America. Her reasons for action in the matter are therefore, it may be said, of a very subordinate kind compared with those that concern us. In America, transportation at the lowest possible cost assumes the attitude of an affair of the highest state necessity.

In view of that state necessity, all local and individual interests must be compelled to give way. How far in future years, when these problems are publicly better understood than at present, it may be found politically expedient to give to the general government a control, with the intention of carrying the principles here indicated into effect, it is needless at present to consider.

Besides the physiological effect of locomotion in thus preventing a permanent impress from Climate, it has moral consequences of no little value. These will be seen if we compare the condition of Europe before the Crusades with its condition subsequently. Vast hordes of men under a fanatical impulse were precipitated upon the Holy Land. Coming indiscriminately from all classes of communities that were scarcely elevated above barbarism, the Crusaders were suddenly brought in contact with people inhabiting countries that for ages had been the seats of civilization. Their ideas were not only enlarged, but their very style of thinking was changed. Whoever escaped the perils of these religious enterprises became, on his return to his native place, an influential and authoritative teacher. There was a weakening of the force of those maxims that heretofore had been a guide, society relieving itself of the stress of former modes of thought. It may be doubted whether that great religious movement known as the Reformation would have been possible had it not been for the occurrence of the Crusades, the precipitation of whatever there was enterprising in Europe upon

Asia. If they did no more, they certainly accelerated its occurrence by several hundred years.

In like manner, the discovery of America by Columbus, the doubling of the Cape by De Gama, and the circumnavigation of the world by Magellan, through the prodigious military and mercantile activity they generated, led to equally important results. Trade, which until then had been chiefly overland or terrestrial, became maritime, a change important in the highest degree, since it eventually gave rise to the prodigious development of manufacturing industry. Heavy masses of goods can never be transported by caravans, though they can easily in ships. The geographical value of countries was changed. Egypt, for instance, lost her position. The commercial arrangements of Europe were completely dislocated. Venice and Genoa were deprived of their mercantile supremacy; prosperity left the Italian towns; the commercial monopolies so long in the hands of the European Jews were broken down. These were the first steps of that maritime development soon exhibited by Western Europe. And since commercial prosperity is forthwith followed by the production of men and the concentration of wealth, and, moreover, implies an energetic intellectual condition, it appeared before long that the three centres of population, of wealth, and of intellect were shifting westwardly. The front of Europe was suddenly changed;

the British Islands, hitherto in a sequestered and eccentric position, were all at once put in the van of the new movement. Wealth poured in, and markets were sought for all over the globe. The separate principalities and kingdoms were taught to act in unison, and the idea of Europe—united Europe—was made manifest.

Life, whether social or personal, is a condition implying movement. Its energy is in proportion to the activity with which interior motions are made. In the animal body the blood circulates through every part, here carrying away worn-out and wasted material, there presenting new substances to accomplish needful repairs. If one region be too hot, the ever-flowing blood bears away with it the excess of temperature; if another be too cold, the blood imparts to it some of its own warmth. In this manner there is a perpetual equalization of differences, a continual restoration of structure. Particles that are in excess at one point are dissolved, and carried to others where they may be of more use.

For the healthy condition of the social system an unceasing movement is also needed. There is an ennui into which a nation may fall. Hence the injunction—move, if it only be for the sake of moving—really conveys a practical good, and in this sense motion may be looked upon not only as a means, but also as an end.

Now, when we consider the position of the American continent—its Atlantic front looking upon Europe, its Pacific front looking upon Asia; when we reflect how much Nature has done for it in the wonderful river system she has bestowed, and how varied are the mineral and agricultural products it yields, it would seem as if we should be constrained by circumstances to carry out spontaneously in practical life the abstract suggestions of policy. A country that stands at the head of all others in its producing power must of necessity continually increase its interior means of motion. Great undertakings, such as the construction of the Pacific Railroad, pressed into existence by commercial motives and fostered for military reasons, will indirectly accomplish political objects not yielding in importance to those that are obvious and avowed.

A few years more, and the influence of the Great Republic will resistlessly extend in a direction that will lead to surprising results. So importunate and increasing is the demand for human labor, so tempting its remuneration, so productive its use, that those stagnant Asiatic tribes to which our attention has in some of these pages been directed, can not fail to be affected. The stream of Chinese emigration already setting into California is but the precursor of the flood that is to come. Here are the fields, there are the men. The dominant Power on the Pacific Ocean must necessarily exert a controlling influence in the affairs of Asia.

The Roman Empire is regarded, perhaps not unjustly, as the most imposing of all human political creations. Italy extended her rule across the eastern and western basins of the Mediterranean Sea, from the confines of Parthia to Spain. A similar central but far grander position is occupied by the American continent. The partitions of an interior and narrow sea are replaced by the two great oceans. But, since History ever repeats itself, the maxims that guided the policy of Rome in her advance to sovereignty are not without application here. Her mistakes may be monitions to us.

A great, a homogeneous, and yet an active people, having strength and security in its political institutions, may look forward to a career of glory. It may, without offense, seek to render its life memorable in the annals of the human race.

## CHAPTER II.

### ON THE EFFECTS OF EMIGRATION.

*Admitting the correctness of the division of Society into three grades, as established by Machiavelli, the effect arising from the emigration of each of those grades is considered, and illustrations from the history of Spain and England examined. The extinction of the Romans and diffusion of the Arabs are traced to their physiological causes.*

*The political consequences of immigration are illustrated by the establishment of the Cotton manufacture in Europe and Negro slavery in America.*

*The ante-historic settlement of Europe by immigrants from Asia, as determined by the modern methods of linguistic research, is next considered, the laws of Population explained in connection therewith, and the necessity of material to moral changes suggested.*

*Machiavelli's principles and the foregoing results are then applied to the United States—1st. European immigration in the North; 2d. Internal emigration to the West; 3d. Prospective emigration to the South; 4th. Asiatic immigration to the Pacific States. The evils contingent on the spread of Polygamy, and the general effects of all these movements on the wealth and grandeur of the Republic, are shown.*

Pressure at home and inducement abroad perpetually incite men to leave their native country and settle in foreign lands.

In considering the effect of such emigrations, we must bear in mind the statement of Machiavelli, that in every great society there are necessarily three orders of men—a superior order, who understand things through their own unassisted mental powers; an intermediate order, who understand things when they are explained to them; a lower order, who do not understand at all. Of the first, it may be added that they are limited in number, but dominant in intelligence; of the second, that in modern countries having free journalism they fall under its influence, the man of this grade adopting the opinions of his accustomed newspaper, and unconsciously retailing them as his own; of the third, which is by far the most numerous, its members pass through life in an intellectual monotonous slumber—they think in monosyllables.

Now, the political effect of emigrations depends upon this condition—from which of those three orders has the emigrating mass issued? We detect the guiding principle at a glance. If the drain has been from the lower or laboring class, the consequent result may not amount to much, for the diminution of that class is capable of quick repair. The self-multiplying force of an old society is, as we shall shortly find, greater than the number realized, which is kept down by resisting influences; and just as the atmosphere will press into an exhausted space, so will that unsatisfied, that restrained power of multiplication quickly fill up the vacancy that has been made.

On the other hand, should the migrating body

have diminished seriously the number of the highest class, the result is a far more important, a far more permanent affair. A loss of the direct influence of these men is no inconsiderable thing; for, no matter what may be the form of government the affected community may live under, they will and do control public thought. Still more, Society has no means of recruiting at its pleasure the wasted ranks of this class. Such individuals come at limited intervals, and only here and there.

History furnishes us with many instructive instances as evidences of these truths.

The discovery of America by Columbus completed that wonderful change in Europe which had been begun by the Crusades. After the German movements that brought the Roman Empire to an end had terminated, the lower strata of population fell into a comparatively quiescent state. From this condition they had not been sensibly disturbed by the political events of the reign of Charlemagne. The Holy Wars may, however, without exaggeration, be said to have precipitated all Europe upon Asia. A very great intellectual change in the whole continent was the result.

The Crusading outrush to the East was followed on the discovery of America by an outrush of adventurers across the Atlantic to the West. Religious sentiment was superseded by avarice. There was not a people in Europe who did not become involved. As might be expected from her position, Spain was profoundly implicated in all her social ranks. Her men of influence in civil life, in military life, in ecclesiastical life, all emigrated across the ocean. The thirst for gold was too strong for even the pride of family. A paradise of unbounded sensual enjoyment in this life, riches exceeding whatever the wildest dreams of fanatical alchemists had ever suggested—a realized El Dorado—these were temptations that the hot Spanish blood could not resist. The melancholy Peruvian Inca, whose brow was adorned with a diadem of scarlet-tasseled fringe, when he stretched out his finger on his prison wall, and promised to give vessels of gold to that height if they would restore him to liberty, only added to the fierce avarice of his tormentors.

What Spain did on this continent can never be too often related—it ought never to be forgotten. She acted with an appalling atrocity to those Indians, as though they did not belong to the human race. Their lands and goods were taken from them by apostolic authority. Their persons were next seized under the text that the heathen are given as an inheritance, and the uttermost parts of the earth for a possession. It was one unspeakable outrage, one unutterable ruin, without discrimination of age or sex. They who died not under the lash in a tropical sun, died in the darkness of the mine. From sequestered sand-banks, where the red flamingo fishes in the gray of the morning—from fever-stricken mangrove thickets and the gloom of impenetrable forests—from hiding-places in the clefts of rocks and the solitude of invisible caves—from the eternal snows of the Andes, where there was no witness but the all-seeing sun, there went up to God a cry of human despair. By millions upon millions, whole races and nations were remorselessly cut off. The Bishop of Chiapa affirms that more than fifteen millions were exterminated in his time. From Mexico and Peru a civilization that might have instructed Europe was crushed out.

The crime of Spain became her punishment. Look at her present state! Where is all that enterprise, that energy, that intelligence, which made her the leading nation of Europe? Lost in the wilds of America, swamped in Indian blood. Has she found it possible to recruit that true intellectual aristocracy she lost? The emigration of her best and bravest wrought her irreparable ruin. The Mexican and Peruvian have had their revenge. There lies the deteriorated country utterly past cure.

In Europe there is another nation that from our present point of view likewise claims our attention. The English have peopled by emigration, within three centuries, very large portions of the surface of

the earth. The drain on that population has been, for the most part, from the second and third classes, the first having been implicated in it but to an insignificant extent. This remark applies even to the extreme case of India, a country that might be supposed to offer very great temptations.

As respects the colonization of North America and Australia, together with the less important points, as South Africa and New Zealand, there was but little inducement for those who prefer a life of learned ease, or who seek by speedy methods social distinction. The work to be accomplished was the hard conquest of Nature, the removing of forests, extracting the fruits of the earth, founding of cities, establishment of trade. On the other hand, in the parent country there was an ancient and firmly seated aristocracy, an established church with great endowments, a law of primogeniture, and the not difficult attainment of eminent distinction by approved talent. In a double manner, then, these circumstances tended to restrain the first class from participating in the movement; and a singular benefit was undoubtedly derived, as we see in the result, for the intrinsic strength of that nation has, beyond question, from these emigrations suffered no decline.

In certain particulars English Emigration resembles the Emigrations from Ancient Greece. Both cases present a restricted territory as the immediate inciting cause, and a tendency to colonization as the form. On the shores of the Mediterranean and Black Seas, from Sinope to Saguntum, were scattered affiliated settlements. These probably were founded on the general principles first adopted by Tyre, a city that led the way in the organization of European, Asiatic, and North African commerce. The wealth accumulated by some of these colonial towns led to such habits of luxury as to excite the wonder of antiquity, and actually to become proverbial. The debaucheries and dissipation of the Sybarites were sustained by their lucrative commerce. This intercolonial trade was chiefly for slaves, mineral products, articles of manufacture, tin, bronze, oil, amber, dyed goods, and worked metals. Position or accident made particular towns the chief marts for special commodities. Thus, Delos was the great dépôt for slaves. It is affirmed that as many as ten thousand were sold there in a single day. Notwithstanding their wealth, none of the Grecian colonies attained the political power of the greatest of the Tyrian colonies, Carthage, which maintained for many years and through many wars a nearly evenly balanced military power with Rome itself.

The intrinsic weakness of such colonial systems is shown by the fate of those of Tyre and Greece. Both were ruined by the policy of Alexander the Great. Though the former city had suffered severely in her

contests with the Babylonian Empire, and Old Tyre had been destroyed after a siege of thirteen years by a Babylonian king, her site being made "as bare as the top of a rock on which the fisherman spreads his nets," and "the isles of the sea were troubled at her departure," the new City had succeeded to much of the commercial prosperity of the Old. It was not from any vindictive spirit, but because he discerned plainly the political power derived through its position, that Alexander resolved on the utter destruction of the place. He took it, after a siege of seven months, by building a mole from the main land to the island on which the town stood. Immediately after the assault, in which a vast multitude of its defenders fell, two thousand of the inhabitants were crucified. With the fall of Tyre the domination of Asia as a Mediterranean power came to an end, and with the foundation of Alexandria came the commercial ruin of Greece.

It is singular how completely these prosperous colonial settlements, with the single exception of Carthage, disappeared politically on the extinction of their commercial centres. Such establishments can never be a source of power to the mother country. If she relies upon them, they will fail her in her hour of need. Founded for the sake of gain, a habit of greed grows upon them—so much that they become unwilling to bear sacrifices, even though obviously for their own good.

What Tyre and Greece were in the Mediterranean Sea, which was almost the world to them, England has been on the greater theatre of the globe. She has founded by emigration colonies in North America, the West Indies, South Africa, Australia, New Zealand, India. In forty-three years, counting from 1815, the close of her wars with France, she sent forth about four and a half millions of souls.

Though the intention of the English in these movements has chiefly been the founding of colonies, the motive has varied at different times. In the case of that which events have proved to have been by far the most important of them all—the Puritan emigration—it was religious sentiment.

For many years the European current of emigration to the United States was comparatively feeble It was mainly derived from England, Ireland, Scotland, and Germany, and continued at a nearly uniform annual rate from the American Revolution until about 1806. From 1784 to 1794 the yearly rate was only about 4000. In the latter year it rose to 10,000, but never recovered that point again until 1817. This falling off was due to the European wars, which not only created an urgent demand for men, both for land and sea service, but also to the enforcement of the principle at that time insisted upon by the English government, that a subject could never throw off his allegiance—"once a subject, always a subject." Experience had led to the conclusion that not much reliance could be placed on the affection a man may spontaneously feel for the country of his birth, an affection arising from the recollections of early life.

In 1817, when the fear of English impressment had passed away, the emigration to the United States rose to 22,240. In this aggregate there were included many native-born Americans, who had, through the accidents of the war, been detained in Europe, and were now returning. Due allowance made for this, the sudden impetus may be traced to the declining demand for men for military and naval purposes, the great derangement in the pursuits of the working-classes as a state of war was exchanged for a state of peace, and the financial disturbances which were occurring or impending.

The current now steadily gathered force. In 36¼ years, ending December 31st, 1855, the United States received nearly four millions and a quarter of immigrants. Among them are found

| | |
|---|---|
| 1,348,682 British. | 747,930 Irish. |
| 1,206,087 Germans. | 34,599 Scotch. |
| 207,492 English. | 188,725 French. |

Under the title "British," in this table, are included English, Scotch, and Irish; their relative proportions can not now be ascertained. Competent authorities have, however, been led to the conclusion that of these at least one million were from Ireland. This would make the total Irish immigration for that period 1,747,930.

From the best estimates now accessible, it appears that the total immigration in the United States, since the Revolution to the close of 1855, has been nearly four and a half millions:

| | |
|---|---|
| Immigrants up to Sept. 30th, 1819 . | 250,000 |
| " " Dec. 31st, 1855 . | 4,212,624 |
| | 4,462,624 |

In a general manner, it may therefore be affirmed that the United States have gained as much from Europe by immigration, as Great Britain has lost from her domestic population by emigration. At the commencement of the civil war the number did not differ much from five millions.

It might be supposed that the English emigration, as was the case with the Greek, originated mainly from over-population at home, but to this cause must unquestionably be added a willing disposition to resort to expatriation. If these movements have been promoted in the British Islands by the facilities arising from the same language being spoken in America, that motive will not apply to the case of Germany as it stands in comparison with that of France. The German immigration has been nearly seven fold that of France. It has long been remarked that the shepherd population, which in ancient times reached from the Baltic to China, was perpetually occupied in warlike migrations, readily uniting itself under chieftains to make incessant attacks on the Asiatic empires, and eventually accomplishing the destruction of the Roman. It kept every thing in a disturbed state. Not until Central Europe became engaged in other pursuits did these commotions cease.

The essential difference between ancient and modern migrations consists in this, that the former were tribal, the latter individual, and, indeed, continually becoming more and more exclusively so. A tribe forcing itself into the seats of its neighbor can only accomplish its purpose by violence, which necessarily provokes resistance. The movements of the Goths, the Huns, the Magyars, the Turks, the Tartars, are cases in point; but where the movement is individual, the intruder is quietly and imperceptibly melted down in the population among whom he has come.

But, though tribal emigration has thus declined into individual, the races that were expansive in the ancient times still continue to be so. In the case of emigration to the United States, the obstruction arising from difference of language applied quite as much to the Germans as to the French. Admitting the great drain there had been upon the latter through their revolutionary and imperial wars, there were certainly as great temptations for them in Canada, as there were for the former in the Union. The Teutons and Saxons have never lost their wandering propensity, though, with the progress of civilization, which has imparted safety and rapidity to individual locomotion, the manner of satisfying it has changed.

This change from tribal to individual emigration tends to restrict the movement to the third social grade. It is by that class that domestic pressure and foreign inducement are most powerfully felt; and hence, though the losses of Great Britain have been numerically so great, her intrinsic strength, as already remarked, has suffered no decline.

The transplantation of men can not be accomplished without physiological modifications ensuing. I may now indicate, in a general manner, the principles governing those modifications.

When, from its original seat, a people is suddenly transposed to some new abode, in which the climate, the seasons, the aspect of Nature are altogether different, it spontaneously commences in all its parts a movement to come into harmony with the new conditions—a movement of a secular nature, and implying the consumption of many generations for its accomplishment. During such a period of transmutation there is, of course, an increased waste of life, a risk, indeed, of total disappearance or national death; but, the change once completed, the requisite correspondence once attained, things go forward again in an orderly manner on the basis of the new modification that has been assumed. When the change to be accomplished is very profound, involving extensive anatomical alterations, not merely in the appearance of the skin, but even in the structure of the skull, long periods of time are undoubtedly required, and many generations of individuals are consumed.

Or, by interior disturbance, particularly by blood admixture, with more rapidity may a national type be affected, the result plainly depending on the extent to which admixture has taken place. This is a disturbance capable of mathematical computation. If the blood admixture is only of limited amount and transient in its application, its effect will sensibly disappear in no very long period of time, though never, perhaps, in absolute reality. This accords with the observation of philosophical historians, who agree in the conclusion that a small tribe intermingling with a larger one will only disturb it in a temporary manner, and after the course of a few years the effect will cease to be perceptible. The incoming stream not only brings its physical peculiarities, but its mental peculiarities too. Its intrinsic force is, however, very far from being as great as might have been anticipated, for its own condition, through climate, is about to change; it has not, therefore, that fixity of purpose and resolution that it possessed in its native seat. The tendency to homogeneousness is all the time felt. It is as if a few drops of water were put into a tumbler of wine, and the water itself gradually turning into wine. In the first moments the admixture might be apparent enough, but it would become indistinguishable at last.

Moreover, as the invaded community gradually grows or expands, the same intrusive volume is of relatively less and less effect.

National homogeneousness is thus obviously secured by the operation of two distinct agencies—the first, gradual but inevitable dilution; the second, motion to come into harmony with the external natural state. The two conspire in their effects.

Homogeneousness in a nation makes it conservative, and secures its internal stability by producing a common direction of thought; for though, of necessity, the different orders of population occupy themselves mentally with different things, it does not follow but that the modes of thinking of all may be alike. Historians have long remarked how strikingly this holds good in the old empires of Asia; and that, though monarchs and their ministers may be punished during political troubles, it never occurs to any one that the system is wrong, or that it needs the slightest change. On the contrary, in Europe the different orders think differently; there is an intrinsic difference between the conclusions of the intelligent few and the fetichisms of the innumerable illiterate mass. This is the cause that on that continent government has become so difficult, and that there is nothing certain as to its right principles, and no unanimity in religion.

The foregoing principles are illustrated in a striking manner by the history of the Romans. From a central nucleus in Italy they spread all round the Mediterranean Sea. Greek, Asiatic, Syrian, Egyptian, African, Spaniard, Gaul, Briton, were all conquered and contaminated by them, and contaminated them in return. But how stood the numerical relation? What was the blood of Italy transfused into all that foreign blood? and what, in the nature of the thing, must become of the Romans? They were literally dissolved and lost in the conterminous races. With them went all their ideas, all their institutions. Their political forms vanished—their religious forms, their paganism, disappeared. On the contrary, the thoughts of the conquered people vanquished the thoughts of the Romans. In the most important of all instances that can be adduced, we see how true this is. Christianity did not originate in Imperial Rome; it was not imposed by her on the provinces. It originated in the provinces, and was by them forced on the reluctant arbitress of the world.

In this mortal adulteration of the true Roman blood there was one particular influence deserving our thoughtful attention. It operated in the very heart of the Empire—in Italy itself. Incredible dissipation, the offspring of enormous riches, sapped society. In the reigns of the first Emperors it was looked upon as a singular felicity to have no family. I can here only touch lightly on that state of things; but whoever will reflect on the subject will see that the matter must have pressed severely on the state before law after law, each more stringent than its predecessor, was enacted to correct the evil. The thing went on from bad to worse, until slave concubinage was almost universal. No language can describe the state of Rome after the civil wars. The accumulation of power and wealth gave rise to a universal depravity. Law ceased to be of any value. A suitor must deposit a bribe before a trial could be had. The social fabric was a festering mass of rottenness. The people had become a populace, the aristocracy was demoniac, the city was a hell. No crime that the annals of human wickedness can show was left unperpetrated. Remorseless murders; the betrayal of husbands, wives, friends; poisoning reduced to a system. Legal marriage had almost ceased. The younger women had become so incredibly extravagant that the men affirmed they could not support them. In the time of Cæsar it was necessary for the government to interfere, and actually put a premium on marriage. He gave rewards to women who had many children; prohibited those who were under forty-five years of age, and who had no children, from wearing jewels and riding in litters, hoping by such social disabilities to correct the evil. Finding that this was of no avail, Augustus, in view of the general avoidance of legal marriage and resort to concubinage with slaves, was compelled to impose penalties on the unmarried—to enact that they should not inherit by will, except from relations. Plutarch emphatically stigmatized the condition when he wrote, "The Romans marry to be heirs, and not to have heirs."

Nations can not be permanently modified except by principles or actions conspiring with their existing tendency. Violence perpetrated upon them passes away, leaving, perhaps, in a few generations, no vestige of itself. Even Victory is conquered by Time. The extinction of Races of men is never accomplished by Force, but by insidious agencies, that modify the men themselves.

Such was the effect as regards the Roman race. It slowly died out in Italy itself; and, particularly after the wars of Justinian, the German tribes flowed in to fill the void. The splendid architecture, the magnificent recollections, the glorious sky, the fields that had been so lately a garden—did these forthwith raise the intruders to the standard of the departed? Changes in the human race take time. For a thousand years the condition of that population was as debased as it is possible for that of a community to be. Meanwhile climate and the aspect of nature were gradually doing their work, and out of such base material the modern Italian arose.

There is a tendency in a hybrid offspring to exhibit a preference for that which may be regarded as the more honorable of its constituents, and this even though the commingling has occurred in a violent way, as by conquest. The barbarian invasions of Italy had in a few centuries in this manner completely amalgamated the remnant of the Roman ethnical element that still remained in the peninsula—so completely, that the old manners were gone, the old religion supplanted, the language dead. Yet the conquering element acknowledged the supremacy of the conquered. It willingly forgot its traditions beyond the Danube, and cherished a delusive pride in the glory of the great republican times.

Blood degeneration implies thought degeneration. As the great statesman to whom I have already referred, himself an Italian, and profoundly appreciating these things, observes, Cæsar and Pompey had disappeared, John, Matthew, and Peter had come in their stead. Barbarized names are the outward and visible signs of barbarized ideas. It was nothing more than might be expected that, in this mongrel race, customs, and language, and even names, should change

—that rivers, and towns, and men should receive new appellations. Nor was it until the Italian population had re-established itself in a physiological relation with the country that manly thoughts and true conceptions could be regained. Ideas and dogmas, that would not have been tolerated for an instant in the pure old homogeneous Roman race, found acceptance in this adulterated, this festering mass.

I will still farther enforce these principles by an illustration scarcely inferior in weight to that furnished by Rome herself.

Hitherto we have been considering Nations, civilized and barbarian, who were animated by ideas that we may strictly term European. But these principles are illustrated with equal emphasis if the communities under examination are Asiatic.

When, under Mohammed and his successors, the Arabians burst forth from their native seats and carried their conquering arms into the heart of Asia on one side, and to the Atlantic Ocean on the other, so rapid was their diffusion, so small their own mass, so prodigious the volume of humanity with which they mixed, that it might have seemed impossible but that an instant fate should overtake them — their conquests ephemeral, themselves vanishing away. But the very reverse occurred. For centuries in succession, the countries they had conquered they held; nay, more, they literally Arabized them.

The explanation of this surprising political result turns altogether on the position of the female sex among Asiatics. In barbarous states the woman is the slave of the man; the Asiatic makes her his toy, the European his companion. The avarice of the former for beauty is replaced in the latter by an avarice for wealth. The treasures of the one are placed in a harem, those of the other are invested in the public funds.

The natural position of the female sex in this respect is indicated at once by the relation of numbers. In Europe, for every 106 male births there are 100 female; hence we may truly affirm that monogamy is the proper condition of our species, and that, apart from its social evils, polygamy is an unnatural state.

But, though this is the scientific conclusion to which we must come, no one can deny the prodigious political power of polygamic institutions. What must be the inevitable result when there were single families sometimes of nearly two hundred children, who were all glorying in their descent from their conquering father and speaking his tongue? Was it to be wondered at that tribute in all the vanquished countries soon ceased, and that the physiognomy and mental constitution of the Arab every where prevailed?

To this, the direct effect of polygamy, we must add the influence of that most ungallant practice of the

Asiatics, the exclusion of their women from society. It cut off effectually what little influence was left. We need not believe them when they say that they do not do this through jealousy; nor need we accept their defamation, that so deeply implanted in the female heart is the love of fashion and novelty, that there is no grotesqueness too surprising for women to imitate; that, if unconfined, they produce a continual change of customs and an unsettled state; and that any community desiring stability and permanence must shut them up.

That is their shameful slander, that their scandalous practice. If they do gain their wished-for stagnation, what is the price they pay?—the family. The monogamous habit makes the family. It leads to the accumulation and transmission of wealth from generation to generation in the same house. With this arises a liability to a concentration of power in castes, and the use of surnames that perpetuate family interests and family pride. In Europe the career of improvement is in the Society, in Asia it is in the Individual. Doubtless, in Asia, there are women who can more than rival the bewitching fascinations of their European sisters—women of exquisite form and of transcendent loveliness. A village in Palestine was the birthplace of the Madonna! But among us there is more than all that—something that they can never see, something that is produced by the family and social relation, for it is therein that the beautiful qualities of our women shine forth. At the close of a long life, checkered with pleasures and misfortunes, how often does the aged man with emotion confess that, though all the ephemeral acquaintances and attachments of his career have ended in disappointment and alienation, the wife of his youth is still his friend! In a world from which every thing else seems to be passing away, her affection alone is unchanged—true to him in sickness as in health, in misfortune as in prosperity, true in the hour of death.

Thus, in the spread of the Arabians, if the sword made the conquest, Polygamy secured it. A social remodeling in all the subjugated countries took effect. There lies the secret of the permanence of the Arab and of the disappearance of the Roman.

Besides the effects here pointed out, the Mohammedan emigration into Europe has left an impression so deep as to impart a characteristic feature to modern civilized life. To those Orientals we must impute the immediate origin of the scientific and industrial pursuits of our own times. Nay, more, their ideas and the consequences of their actions, both for evil and for good, have tinctured the daily life of America. An art introduced by the Arabians into Spain was the inciting cause of the great development of the Slave system in the United States—that system for the sake of which the civil war was provoked. For, though in one respect the growth and manufacture of cotton may be said to be indigenous here, since fabrics of that material were extensively used by the Mexicans at the time of the conquest by Cortez, it was not the spread of this, but of the European cotton industry, that has affected the Southern States so profoundly.

It is scarcely possible to refer to a more striking instance of the impression that may be made by the habits of emigrants on the communities in which they have resided. The Moors have long ago been removed from Spain, but the arts they there introduced have spread to other countries, and permanently influenced their life.

It has sometimes been asked, not without an air of triumph, where are the proofs of our indebtedness to the Mohammedans, and especially to the Moorish invaders of Spain? It has likewise been asserted that the Saracenic mind never rose above mere commentatorship upon Greek originals in matters of science, and in matters of art was altogether barren and worthless. So far as science is concerned, I have elsewhere shown how untrue and unjust such a statement is, and that, in reality, the scientific knowledge of modern Europe is the offspring of the conquest of Spain; that it was a boon not only received with reluctance, but actually resisted with bitterness by our forefathers, because its fundamental principles were supposed to be in opposition to their habits of thought and interests. And now, as respects industrial art, in the midst of the miracles in which we live, and which, within the last century, has not only figuratively, but in reality, revolutionized the face of the earth, the same assertion may be made. To the Saracens we are indebted for the cotton manufacture. Through their influence that art was extended from Japan to the Gulf of Guinea, from the Pyrenees to the equinoctial line. They spread the use of that material which at this day constitutes a chief source of the wealth of manufacturing Europe and of agricultural America. As in the sciences—mathematics, astronomy, chemistry, etc.—they have left an indelible impression, of which such words as algebra, almanac, alcohol, and many others that might be mentioned, are the enduring reminiscences, so in this branch of industry there are like witnesses: not a few of its terms that have been incorporated in our speech are of Oriental origin. The word cotton itself is Arabic; muslin is so called from Mosul, a city on the banks of the Tigris, where was once the chief seat of its manufacture; calico, from Calicut, in India. The under-garment worn by ladies passes under a name which shows from whom they derived it, for chemise is an Arabic word.

The cotton manufacture was commenced in Spain

by Abderahman III. about A.D. 930, a period during which attention seems to have been particularly directed by the Moors to the improvement of agriculture and manufactures, while the rest of Europe was falling deeper and deeper into barbarism and night. The Khalif introduced into the peninsula the sugar-cane, rice, the mulberry-tree, with many improvements in such arts as tanning and the manufacture of silk. Cotton was carried into Sicily by the Saracens on their occupancy of that island, and, indeed, from Spain the use of it spread more or less all over the north and east of Europe. One of the Mohammedan applications of this vegetable product was destined to be of the utmost value: it was the invention of cotton paper. The real merit of the invention of the art of printing lies not, as is commonly supposed, in the contrivance of the press and types, but in the making of paper. The process of multiplying impressions by seals and stamps, which is essentially a printing process, had been known from the remotest antiquity; but such operations could never be made available for the extensive dissemination of knowledge until something more abundant and cheaper than papyrus and parchment was discovered. This want was supplied by the Arabian cotton paper. A charter of Roger, king of Sicily, A.D. 1102, is expressly stated to have been written on that substance, and, in fact, there are traces of its use somewhat earlier.

The Moors also made paper of linen long before it was known in any other part of Europe.

But, though cotton was resorted to as an article of clothing by the Arabs from the earliest times (from the Khalif downward they wore dresses of it), there was another Oriental nation who greatly excelled them in the perfection of its manufacture. Long before the Macedonian invasion the Hindoos had practiced this art, and to our own times have maintained so great an excellence in it, that those familiar with the most recent improvements still speak of their work with admiration. "It is so beautifully fine," says one, "that it looks like the work of insects or fairies." Another states that he has seen an entire dress made of it drawn through a small ring; that the spinners can make threads so fine as to be hardly discernible—that you can not feel them with the finger; that when the cloth has been laid on the grass to bleach, and the dew has fallen on it, it is actually impossible to see it, justifying the designation that has been applied to it—a web of woven wind; or the condemnation once passed upon it by some of the manufacturers interested in fabrics of a coarser sort, that it was "the mere shadow of a commodity." In the course of innumerable ages, by the practice of this art in successive generations, so exquisite has the sense of touch in the Hindoo spinner become, that he can extend a single grain of cotton into a yarn twenty-nine yards in length, or one pound into more than 115 miles. However, it must be added that the automatic engines of the English factories have excelled that tenuity. At the Great Exhibition there was a sample answering to 1026 miles. In India, the machinery both for spinning and weaving is of the simplest kind, the personal tact of the operative supplying every want, and that often under the most disadvantageous circumstances. Beneath a shed or under the shade of a tamarind-tree the Hindoo fixes his clumsy loom, with every drawback from the oppressiveness or inclemency of the weather. There is in the production of this textile fabric something congenial to his habits; a sedentary life is in correspondence to the climate, and his personal organization is more favorable to delicate tact than to muscular exertion. He shows little disposition to avail himself of obvious improvements which would greatly shorten his labor, preferring to work in the same way that his forefathers did. It should nevertheless be remembered that the spinning-wheel is his invention, and it is no insignificant improvement on the old spindle and distaff. With all the disadvantage of this mental carelessness and immobility, the Mohammedans managed to spread the Hindoo cotton manufacture into the Chinese Empire; and it is by no means uninteresting to notice, as showing the sameness of human nature in all countries, that this intrusion of the cotton manufacture was resisted by the silk interest among the Chinese upon the same principle and in the same way as by the woolen interest in England. Indeed, nearly all the European governments, under the influence of similar motives, either restricted or prohibited the use of cotton goods; and yet, in spite of all such combinations, legislation, and opposition, those fabrics have forced their way until they constitute the chief article of clothing of the human race.

It is sometimes remarked, as a proof of the inferiority of the Asiatics, that this important manufacture remained among them undeveloped and unimproved for more than four thousand years; whereas, when the English took it up, they carried it in less than a century to so great a degree of perfection, that a man could do more work in a day than he had formerly done in a year. Simultaneously other inventions of the most momentous interest to civilization were introduced—the Canal system, the Steam-engine in all its forms, stationary and locomotive, high pressure and low, Railroads, the development of the Iron manufacture, and new methods for rendering all kinds of machinery more exact in construction and perfect in operation.

But I do not think that this inertness in India and this activity in England are to be interpreted in the way such writers suppose. Doubtless the position of women in the social system of India had no little to do with the result. An extensive introduction of machinery never fails to touch domestic life. Even in England the various riots attending the introduction of the manufactures were mainly incited by the apprehension that machinery was throwing the operatives out of work. Extraneous circumstances thus not only arrest, but often enough destroy human occupations. It is upon such principles that we must explain the total destruction of this very manufacture in Spain after the expulsion of the Moors. The Spanish Christian was not inferior to the Spanish Mohammedan. Our reflections on the Hindoos for their incapacity in these improvements are of about as little weight as were those of the woolen weavers brought over to England by Edward III. It was said that the English knew no more what to do with wool than the sheep on whose backs it grew. And this was on the eve of their great development of that branch of industry.

To the Saracens we must therefore attribute the introduction of cotton and the cotton manufacture into Europe. It found its way into England under circumstances in many respects interesting. After the capture of Antwerp by the Duke of Parma in 1585, great numbers of workmen fled to England to escape the sanguinary persecutions. Among these were many cotton artisans, who settled in Manchester, and were kindly received and patronized by the authorities of that town. In the course of the next hundred and fifty years the manufacture had become firmly established, and a considerable cotton trade had arisen with the Levant. In the early part of the last century the demand for these goods had become so considerable that hand-labor had begun to be insufficient to satisfy it, and it was necessary to resort to machinery.

In succession there appeared Wyatt's invention for spinning by pairs of rollers turning with different velocities, Paul's rotary carding engine, Arkwright's great improvements, Hargreaves's jenny, Crompton's mule, and many other contrivances of singular power and beauty.

By these admirable inventions the cotton manufacture underwent so great a development as to require an entire change in its economical management, and hence arose the Factory System. The necessity for this was due, at first, partly to the use of water-power for driving machinery, mills springing up wherever suitable water-power existed; in part, also, to the obvious saving of time, trouble, and money when all the operations are conducted under one roof and under one supervision, instead of being managed, as they formerly were, in a disconnected way, in cottages at a distance from one another.

Though these great improvements in spinning had taken place, the cotton manufacture could not have attained its present surprising extent had it not been for the contemporaneous invention of the steam-engine — contemporaneous, for Watt's first patent was taken out in 1769, the same year that Arkwright patented spinning by rollers. Watt's improvements chiefly consisted in the use of a separate condenser, and the replacement of atmospheric pressure by that of steam. Still, it was not until 1790 that the steam-engine was introduced into factories, and hence it was not, as is commonly supposed, the cause of their wonderful increase. It came, however, at an opportune moment, its use in this application being nearly coincident with the invention of the dressing machine by Radcliffe, and the power-loom by Cartwright.

In other respects there were many happy incidents. If the mechanical department of the cotton manufacture received great advantages from the invention of the steam-engine, its chemical department was equally favored by the discovery of bleaching by chlorine, an application made by Berthollet in 1785, and brought into practical use by Watt. To bleach a piece of cotton by the action of the air and sun had required from six to eight months, and a large surface of land must be used as bleach-fields. The value of land in the vicinity of large towns offered an insuperable obstacle to such uses. Much of the products of the British looms was therefore sent over to Holland to be whitened. The use of dilute sulphuric acid by Dr. Home, of Edinburgh, in the stead of sour milk, hitherto employed in the operation, reduced the time greatly, but still it required three or four months. By chlorine the operation could be completed in the course of a few hours, the fibre being perfectly whitened, its coloring material so thoroughly destroyed as to be altogether incapable of restoration. It was at first used as a watery solution, subsequently as chloride of lime. Nor were the new chemical operations restricted to the bleaching of this fabric. Calico printing, an art practiced many thousand years ago among the Egyptians, as described by Pliny, was also perfected. The Arabs had introduced printing by blocks of wood, an advance on the Indian operation of painting by hand. The great European improvement was printing by cylinders, introduced by Bell in 1785.

As the result of these various inventions, the cotton manufacture in much less than a century had reached such an extension as might almost appear incredible. Mr. Baines, writing in 1833, estimates the total annual value of the manufacture at about one hundred and fifty millions of dollars; the number of persons supported by it at one and a half million; the length of yarn spun at nearly five thousand millions of miles—sufficient to pass round the earth's circumference more than two hundred thousand times —sufficient to reach fifty-one times from the earth to the sun. "It would encircle the earth's orbit eight and a half times. The wrought fabrics of cotton exported in one year would form a girdle for the globe passing eleven times round the equator. The receipts of the manufacturers and merchants for this one production of national industry are equal to two thirds the whole public revenue of the kingdom. To complete the wonder, this manufacture is the creation of the genius of a few humble mechanics. It has sprung up from insignificance to its present magnitude within little more than half a century, and it is still advancing with a rapidity of increase that defies all calculation of what it shall be in future ages."

But such a vast improvement in this particular manufacture necessarily implied other improvements, especially in locomotion and the transmission of intelligence. The peddler's pack, the pack-horse, and the cart, became altogether inadequate, and in succession were replaced by the canal system of the last century, and by the steamboats and railroads of this. The engineering triumphs of Brindley, whose canals were carried across valleys, over or through mountains, above rivers, exacted unbounded admiration in his own times, and yet they were only the precursors of the railroad engineering of ours. As it was, the canal system proved to be inadequate to the want, and oaken railroads, which had long been used in quarries and coal-pits with the locomotive invented by Murdock in 1784, were destined to supplant them.

It does not fall within my present purpose to relate how the locomotion of the whole civilized world was revolutionized, not by the act of some great statesman, or through the power of some mighty sovereign or soldier, but by George Stevenson, once a locomotive stoker, who, by the invention of the tubular boiler, and the ingenious device of blowing the chimney instead of the fire, converted the locomotive of the last century, which at its utmost speed could travel seven miles an hour, into the locomotive of this, which can accomplish seventy. I need not dwell on the collateral improvements—the introduction of iron for the rails, metallic bridges, tubular bridges, viaducts, and all the prodigies of the existing system of railway engineering.

It would demand a work of many volumes to furnish a full and satisfactory description of the industrial improvements of the last century; those we have been considering are, however, quite sufficient to give us a clear appreciation of the direction in which, during that period, the movement tended, and the extent to which it advanced. All that was thus taking place was the necessary result of the material philosophy of the preceding age; the carrying into practice the mechanical ideas introduced by the schools of Galileo and Newton, and these were the direct descendants of the Spanish Mohammedans; for the discoveries of those philosophers had not only been popularized and brought down to the common apprehension, but a growing taste for such pursuits had very generally arisen. We see this in the many modifications of standard experiments in natural philosophy, as those connected with the air-pump, and interesting or amusing applications of electricity. The books of those times are full of interesting instances of the kind, some of which are still employed in our lecture-rooms, or are retained in our elementary works. Such a taste for experimental arrangements and mechanical contrivances was of course powerfully invigorated when there was added an expectation of gaining thereby immense wealth. It was the same principle which had formerly offered an incentive to the alchemists, now, however, directed to objects more easily comprehended, and occupying itself with principles readily understood. If we were to record all the ingenious contrivances originating among men of humble station and means during the last century for the purpose of solving one mechanical problem — that of the perpetual motion— they would form quite a considerable volume. When such tastes had become common, it was not at all surprising that they should be directed to ordinary objects or the operations of daily life, and that an ingenious cottager, who supported his family by spinning, should turn his talent to account by inventing a machine with which one person could spin eight or ten threads at a time instead of one, as by the old-fashioned, time-honored spinning-wheel.

Moreover, when it appeared, from the case of Arkwright and others, that success in this particular direction was the high road to wealth, public consideration, and honor, the realization of riches greater than the wildest tales of the alchemists had ever fabled, an impetus was given, arising from the strongest passion which can animate man. It signified nothing if of the projectors and inventors ninety-nine out of a hundred miserably failed; the splendid success of the hundredth was encouragement enough, and thus from year to year the number of inventions and inventors kept on perpetually increasing, no human pursuit, no object of human interest escaping, and so it continues to our own time.

In this intellectual activity lay the essential progress of the last century. Connected with it there were certain collateral incidents of no little significance. For the first time in her history, overpopulation began to be heard of in England. Even at a period much later, the bearing of these things was altogether misunderstood by men of great intellectual powers and of eminent position. Comparing France with England in the struggle in which he was engaged, Napoleon said, "We must overpower her in the end, for we have a vastly greater population." He overlooked the fact, which at last settled the contest, that her steam-engines were representing at that moment a population of thirty additional millions of adult men; nay, more, men who consumed nothing and produced every thing—men whose only want was a little oil and coal, but who could do without food and clothing, who were indeed ready to find clothing for the whole world, who could labor night and day, who required no sleep, and could not be fatigued. It was not the armies at Waterloo, but these iron men whom he so strangely overlooked in his calculation, that terminated the contest against him. It was through these children of Watt that, after all her taxation, all her subsidies, all her extravagance, all her losses, all her debt, all the inconceivable fatuity of her politicians, England came out of that deadly conflict richer, greater, more vigorous and powerful, than she had ever been before.

If mechanical invention has made so profound an impression on the national life of Europe, it has done the same in America. In the political consequences that have ensued from it, Whitney's gin, invented in 1793, does not yield in importance to the greatest of English inventions. The vast development of the cotton culture in the Southern States, the increased value of negro slave labor, have been its immediate results. The product of cotton furnished from those states in 1856 was estimated at seven-eighths that of the whole world. It amounted in 1860 to more than four millions and a half of bales (4,675,770).

The first African slaves brought to America were imported in a Dutch vessel, which landed them at Jamestown, in Virginia, in 1620. The cultivation of cotton is stated to have been commenced the following year, and from this time the supply of negroes continually increased. It is estimated that in the course of one hundred and fifty-six years, about three hundred thousand slaves had been brought from Africa. An attempt was also made to reduce the native Indians to bondage, but it met with but little success. They did not submit to their fate with the resignation of the blacks. Indeed, at a much later period, it was a subject of remark on the plantations that the slave families in which there was an infusion of Indian blood were characterized by their treacherous and revengeful spirit. Notwithstanding the profits arising from their labor, there was a growing disposition to put some restraint on the importation of slaves. Several of the colonies remonstrated against the trade, but, in opposition to their wishes, the mother country encouraged it. In 1774 the Continental Congress resolved that the importation should be stopped; but in 1789, at the formation of the Constitution, Congress was prohibited from interdicting it until 1808, when it was abolished. Ten years previously (1798), Georgia had set the example of its prohibition. In 1820, Congress passed a law declaring the slave-trade to be piracy.

From evidence which necessarily must be very imperfect, and therefore unreliable, it has been estimated that forty millions of slaves have been taken from Africa. The number imported into the American colonies up to 1776 has been set down at three hundred thousand. The following table gives the slave population from 1790 to 1860:

| Year. | Slave Population. | Year. | Slave Population. |
|---|---|---|---|
| 1790 | 697,879 | 1830 | 2,009,043 |
| 1800 | 893,041 | 1840 | 2,487,455 |
| 1810 | 1,191,364 | 1850 | 3,204,313 |
| 1820 | 1,538,038 | 1860 | 3,952,801 |

From this it appears that the increments are not quite equal to what they should have been if measured by the standard of the white races on the admission of an unrestrained generative action. The resistances which have kept the number down are undoubtedly to be sought for in the unfavorable social circumstances of Southern slave life. It is to be observed that the increase for the decade ending in 1840 is below the mean.

The degree of blood contamination undergone by the negroes is shown by the number of the mulattoes being one ninth that of the blacks. As might be expected, the number of free mulattoes is greater than that of free blacks. The fact is a testimony to the force of instinctive parental feelings.

In slave life the proportion of women to men is above the European mean. The subjoined table shows the number of women to 100 men in the places designated:

| | |
|---|---|
| New England States | 101.41 |
| Southern | 97.04 |
| Middle | 95.88 |
| Southwestern | 91.22 |
| Northwestern | 91.02 |
| Slaves in Southern | 95.90 |
| Europe | 94.34 |

The mean for the entire white American population is about 95.31. The ratio of the female slaves is therefore slightly above that of the white women. The close approach of the numbers is a very interesting physiological fact.

A population of four millions of colored slaves presented, at the commencement of the civil war, a social element that could not be regarded but with the most profound interest. Experience has, however, shown how great a change has been impressed upon the African character by Climate, Blood-admixture, and Ideas. The course these persons have taken must be admitted by all impartial observers as in the highest degree honorable to them.

To the foregoing instances, which serve as illustrations of the general principle we have under consideration, may very profitably be added some of the recent discoveries respecting the settlement of the European continent by its present dominant race—the Indo-European—heretofore briefly referred to (page 40). These will afford an opportunity not only of showing the precision of such pre-historic researches in the hands of modern critics, but also of indicating the general principles of the production and dissemination of a population, of the stages of its progress in civilization, and of the modes by which its manner of life may be affected.

Attempts have often been made to discover the primitive history of nations through the nature and structure of their languages; for since to each well-marked group of men there appertains a specific form of speech, historical relationships may be detected through similarities of language, and this both by the occurrence of similar roots in their vocabularies and by analogies in their grammar. A language, being the creation of a group of men, is developed with their development, declines with their decay, and dies out with their inevitable extinction, unless, as in a few cases, such as the Latin, the Pali, the Prakrit, it is retained by the learned for the literature it contains, or, through ecclesiastical policy, is made sacred. In some respects, therefore, the history of a language corresponds to that of the nation by which it is spoken; though the general mechanism of all languages must present certain features in common, because those features depend on the mechanism of the human mind, which is every where of the same nature.

From a critical study of any existing form of speech, the more important connections and incidents of the people by whom it is spoken may be detected—a criticism which must, however, be pursued in a very guarded manner, and with a clear perception of these accidental, or rather natural coincidences, both as respects the names of things and grammatical structure. It has often been suggested to Comparative Philologists that birds in distant countries, which could never have had any communication with one another, sing not only the same note, but also the same strain; and that a like thing may be observed of cats and dogs, their natural intonations being, however, liable to change through the circumstances of their life. Thus the wild dog never barks, and when the domestic dog relapses into the wild state, it is affirmed that he loses therewith the habit of barking.

In man, similitudes of expression are liable to occur, even in distant places that have never been in intercommunication, particularly in the case of such sounds as have an instinctive origin, as those of weeping, laughter, the exclamations of pain, surprise, joy. Attention being paid to this, there can be no doubt that, by an examination of the language of a people, many facts in its history may be detected, as its intermingling and conflicts with other people, though in this respect the impression of languages upon each other follows the law observed to hold good in the impression of races upon each other, the predominant race apparently extinguishing the other, unless the action should have been very profound.

From such evidence, it appears that, long before the Historic times, the Indo-Europeans, leaving their original country in Asia, migrated through Europe in a northwesterly direction, pressing before them the aborigines of that continent, who receded until they were stopped by the sea, the Finnish and Basque dialects being among the vestiges of that ancient population. These dialects offer indubitable evidence of the small advance in civilization those people had made, and of their mediocre intellect. That the Basque language was in intermediate times spoken from the Alps to the west of Spain, appears to be satisfactorily established from the names which places and other geographical objects still bear. The imperfect communication kept up between different parts of the invading column, as they began to settle and to multiply in the conquered countries, is shown by the diversity of speech, and the introduction of new words occurring in regions at no very great distance from each other. Thus we may infer the chief features of the old belief from the names of certain Greek and Latin gods, and their connection with those of India. For instance, the God of the Sky was called by the Greeks Zeus-pater, by the Latins Jupiter, and in the Veda Dyauspiter. A great many of the classical legends are also to be found in the sacred books of India.

It may also be remarked that this irruption of the Indo-Europeans took place to the southeast as well as to the northwest. Invading Hindostan, they forced the aborigines thereof toward the sea-coast, and even compelled them to escape to the islands beyond. Between these expelled people and the Australian population, as well as the aborigines of Europe, some singular connections have been traced.

The religion of the Autochthons of Europe was a mere worship of Fetishes, and such deities as they had were representatives of natural objects. Probably there were no individuals set apart as priests and no organized ceremonial. As ever will be the case under such circumstances, the base native religion imparted some of its features to its conquering invader, the traces of which may not only be recognized in the theological systems of Greece and Rome, but have even plainly descended to our own times, and that not in mere rural superstitions, but extending to those of a far more important kind. Of such an effect we see a striking example in the case of Ancient Egypt, in which the Fetish worship and adoration of animals by the native Africans became inseparably commingled with the theological conceptions of the conquering intruders long before the epoch of Moses, and the Pharaonic religion, at once noble and base, philosophical and barbarous, was the result.

There is nothing strange in the perpetuation of ideas and modes of thought through many thousand years. Their origin is in the very organization of men; for it is through organization that isolated nations manifest a proclivity to certain mental conceptions and even modes of expression. The negro is essentially a Fetish worshiper—a believer in witchcraft and in the efficacy of charms. Such ideas and the modes of expressing them are found wherever that low grade of humanity occurs, occupying a zone across all Africa and the vast expanse of the Pacific Ocean; nay, even all round the world, if the black populations of America are included; for these in the United States, in the midst of moral, religious, Christian communities, are still full of their African ideas. I believe that if it were possible for a new race of autochthonic negroes to arise, it would inevitably fall into these delusions; as certainly as, if there were new autochthons of the yellow race, they would spontaneously and inevitably invent a monosyllabic language. These are the results of organization. They make their appearance wherever the element of that organization occurs; or, to use a common though perhaps incorrect expression, they descend with the blood. The Finnish peasant still has faith in incantations and charms; he believes that there are witches who can ride on a stick to the moon, and cause her eclipse by their nocturnal invocations; that there are men who can still sell to the sailor a favorable wind, and to the rustic a refreshing shower. It was this element in the blood of Europe that made the barbarian races, after the death of the Latin tongue, such a ready receptacle for all kinds of imposture; that gave faith in relics and force to fetishisms; that turned the minister of the Gospel into a rain-maker and wind-raiser, as if the unchangeable and eternal laws of nature might be suspended or modified at his prayer. It is this which, even in our times, perpetuates the by no means insignificant traces of these ancient delusions. What is thus planted in the very bodily structure, it is hard, if not impossible, altogether to tear up by the roots. Here and there, whenever a favorable moment occurs, it shoots forth again.

Moreover, modern critics have remarked that, as nations are thus distinguished by language, so likewise they are by their culture of art, some imitating, some inventing, but others being incapable of expressing their ideas either by the pencil or in stone. The mental physiognomy of a people is thus so completely shadowed forth, that from the style of a work we instantly detect its origin. The rigid, motionless Egyptian forms betray to us their authors, and this irrespective of what might be termed national blunders, such as the front view of the eye in profiles, and the false position of the ear. And as none of the surrounding nations ever adopted the language of Egypt, so none ever adopted her hieroglyphic system of writing or the peculiarities of her art. Such as they were they remained in their birthplace, and for thousands of years were perfectly stationary, making not the slightest exhibition of an advance. The adjacent Shemitic race possessed no tendency to pictorial expression, their theological systems forbidding the making of graven forms, though this injunction perhaps arose from their insensibility to the embodiment of the beautiful; for it may be doubted whether it is possible, when a tendency to pictorial expression exists, to restrain it by legal penalties.

But how different it was with the Indo-Europeans, a race which, without hesitation, plunged into the depths of metaphysical speculation, and created systems of Philosophy false and true. While, among the Egyptians, many centuries of that leisure which arises from a profound political repose were never illustrated by the improvement of Art, the apathy of Africa perfectly neutralizing all vestiges of the genius of that ancient conquering race, who first brought civilization to the banks of the Nile—while, also, among the Shemites, wealth, luxury, a life of ease, never led to a spontaneous invention of even the first principles of art, very different was it with the Indo-Europeans, whose mental proclivities are every where manifested in architecture and sculpture. It was, however, the Hellenic branch of that race who carried Art to the highest pitch to which it has ever yet attained. Commencing with imperfect beginnings, we see how, among the Greeks, it soon gained a great expansive force, rising degree by degree to the embodiment of those exquisite conceptions of which the sculptures of the Parthenon are the witnesses, and gaining so intense a vitality as to survive Roman conquest and oppression. It was its noble peculiarity that, basing itself on a strict anthropomorphism, it carried out with a rigorous consistency that principle. The remark is perfectly true, that while the Oriental artist expressed his ideas of strength or swiftness by giving to his statue a multitude of arms or of limbs, and thereby made a monster, the Greek, true to his principle and true to man, developed with exquisite tact those human features with which such qualities are connected. His statue was the ideal conception of whatever there is in man essential to strength, or majesty, or beauty, carried into material execution, and prefiguring to us the forms which we should expect that even God himself would have produced had he been pleased to render those qualities incarnate. The Greek made no monsters, but human forms of transcendent perfection. It has been affirmed that this intense idealism rendered him incapable of the execution of portraits, which are best made by men of a realistic turn. His influence in imparting to others his own capability in this respect depended on their natural approach to his own mental peculiarity. Greek art accompanied Greek blood; and as the latter was eliminated from races with whom it had been mingled, and who had thereby gained the power of Greek expression, so do their works exhibit declining stages, and eventually become barbarous and rude.

Such considerations indicate that from a study of the works of art of nations, as from a study of the nature and structure of their languages, incidents in their history may with certainty be determined; conclusions which, when they otherwise accord with the subsequent career of such people, and in the determination of which, if sufficient care and skill have been employed, may be received as indubitable, although they may relate to pre-historic times.

Migrating thus from Central Asia, the column of invaders destined to give birth to the permanent population of Europe encountered, in the new seats to which they gradually advanced, many diversities of climate. In accordance with the principles set forth on foregoing pages, they thereby underwent physiological changes in complexion and bodily construction. Various national types were thus produced.

He who accepts the doctrine of the unity of the human race—that is, its origination from one primordial pair—must, in view of the numerous modified forms of men now dispersed all over the surface of the earth, assign an almost paramount control to climate and to modes of life; but the conclusion to which he is compelled, if broadly stated, would doubtless be very reluctantly received. Its apparent extravagance may, however, serve to give emphasis to the physiological principle involved; for on those principles it would follow that if the life of a man could be prolonged through many centuries, and he were to occupy it in making a journey over the earth from the Arctic to the Antarctic Circle, though he might have been perfectly white at first, his complexion would in succession pass through every degree of darkness, and by the time he had reached the equator, toward the middle of his life, he would be perfectly black. Continuing his journey, his color would lighten as he proceeded, and on his reaching the Antarctic he would become pale again, all these changes occurring without any loss of his personal identity. Moreover, in this his progress, supposing that his mode of life, as regards food and comfort, was such as natural conditions suggest, even his skull would vary, and with it his intellectual powers.

His forehead, reclining at the outset, would undergo rectification as he slowly advanced to more genial climes; the facial angle enlarging and reaching a maximum at the time of his residence in the temperate zone, but diminishing again, and his countenance becoming baser, as he approached the equator, the receding aspect being then for the second time assumed. Still passing onward toward the south, the facial angle would again enlarge, the skull re-rectifying, the intellectual powers expanding, and this condition attaining its perfection in the midst of the south temperate zone, a relapse ensuing as the Antarctic Circle was gained, and there, for the third time, the reclining skull being assumed. Nor is this all; for if, in this his career, children were born to him, they would be of every shade of color and of every form of skull, for such existing physical peculiarities are capable of hereditary transmission. I have said that this illustration may be supposed extravagant; philosophically, however, on the doctrine referred to, it is not so; for what else than such an imaginary prolonged individual life is the life of a race? and what more has thus occurred to the imaginary traveler than has actually happened to the human family?

If such are the effects that would ensue to an emigrant slowly passing along a meridional track, the case would be quite different if the movement were along a parallel of latitude. In this direction the variations of climate are far less marked, and depend much more on geographical than on astronomical causes. In emigrations of this kind there is never that rapid change of aspect, complexion, and intellectual power which must occur in the other. Thus, though the mean temperature of Europe increases from Poland to France, chiefly through the influence of the great Atlantic current transferring heat from the Gulf of Mexico and tropical ocean, that rise is far less than what would be encountered on passing through the same distance to the South. By the arts of civilization man can much more easily avoid the difficulties arising from variations along a parallel of latitude than those upon a meridian, for the simple reason that in that case those variations are less.

The Indo-European emigrating body, thus forcibly intruding itself into every region of Europe, not only came under the influence of the laws of Climate, but also of those laws that determine the increase and diminution of Population; for though, doubtless, the birth and death of every human being is, in a religious sense, the appointment of Heaven, politically the subject has to be regarded from a less dignified point of view. Population is determined by Law.

The population of old countries exhibits secular variations, sometimes increasing and sometimes diminishing. These variations often stand in such a connection with political events as to be plainly their consequences. The population of the whole Roman Empire was prodigiously affected by the introduction of Christianity; that of Italy was reduced by the wars of Justinian. The north of Africa was almost depopulated by the effects of theological quarrels, but it was restored again by the influence of Mohammedanism. The introduction of the feudal system put a premium on the production of men, and accordingly vast numbers appeared. The Crusades gave rise to a diminution. From the eleventh to the sixteenth century, during five hundred years, the population of England did not double; but in fifty years after 1790, it doubled in spite of great wars; and that this was owing to a local cause is clear, from the simultaneously stationary condition of many other countries.

Owing to the diminution of causes which will presently be explained as resisting agencies, the annual increase of the United States in population has been nearly three times as much as that of Prussia, including her gains from the partition of Poland; four times as much as that of Russia; six times that of Great Britain; nine times that of Austria; ten times that of France.

Again, the geographical centre of Population is liable to displacement. Thus, the centre for Europe has passed to the north of its ancient position since the fall of Paganism. The establishment of the Feudal system occasioned one dislocation of it, the development of manufacturing industry in the northwest of Europe another.

In the United States the direction of increase by population is nearly due west. "The centre of representative population of the Union in 1840 was in the northwestern extremity of Virginia. It had traveled westward since 1790, when it was in Baltimore County, Maryland, 182 miles distant, in very nearly the same parallel of latitude."

Montesquieu expresses an opinion which doubtless would be strenuously objected to in our day if advanced otherwise than facetiously: "A man is worth what he will sell for; in some countries he is worth nothing, in others less than nothing." From this it would seem to follow, that if production depends upon demand, population will be affected by those well-known laws holding good in the case of other commodities.

Leaving the consideration of that aspect of the case to the ingenuity of the reader, it may be asserted as being beyond contradiction that not only is population determined by physical agencies, but also by human legislation or the policy of governments; for governments, by such obvious means as voluntarily engaging in wars, can occasion an absolute diminution through the destruction of life that ensues, and they may also, by their course of policy, diminish the number of births. They ought to be just as much held accountable for restraining the appearance of individuals as for destroying them after they have appeared.

We can have no better example of the control exercised by public policy over population than the condition of things in Rome after the Civil Wars. The existence of the State was in danger. It has been mentioned (page 109) how an indisposition to contract matrimony had arisen. Laws were enacted to correct the evil, but with so little success that it became necessary to resort to other means for increasing the population. Tacitus, speaking of the reign of Claudius, says: "The line of those families which were styled by Romulus the first class of nobility, and by Brutus the second, was almost extinct. Even those of more recent date, created in the time of Julius Cæsar by the Cassian Law, and under Augustus by the Senian, were well-nigh exhausted." Under these circumstances, the Emperor, in a speech of remarkable ability, advocated the introduction of prominent nobles even into the Senate. "My ancestors, the oldest of whom, Attus Clausus, though of Sabine origin, was at once enrolled among Roman citizens and adopted into the patrician rank, furnish me with a lesson that I ought to pursue similar measures in directing the affairs of the commonwealth, and transfer to Rome every thing that is of pre-eminent merit wheresoever found. Nor, indeed, am I ignorant that from Alba we had the Julii, from Camerium the Coruncanii, and the Portii from Tusculum; and, not to enter into a minute detail of remote transactions, that from Etruria, Lucania, and all Italy persons have been incorporated into the Senate. At last our city became bounded only by the Alps, so that not only separate individuals, but whole states and nations, were ingrafted into the Roman name. We had solid peace at home, and our arms prospered abroad, when the nations beyond the Po were presented with the rights of citizens; and when, under pretext of leading out our legions into colonies all over the earth, and uniting with them the flower of the natives, we recruited our exhausted state. Do we regret that the Balbi migrated to us from Spain, or men equally illustrious from the Narbon Gaul? Their descendants remain yet with us, nor yield to us in their love of this our common country. What proved the bane of the Spartans and Athenians, though potent in arms, was that they treated as aliens and refused to unite with the conquered. On the other hand, so great was the wisdom of Romulus our founder, that he saw several people his enemies and his citizens in one and the same day. Foreigners have even reigned over us. For magistracies to be intrusted to the children of freemen is no innovation, as many are erroneously persuaded, but a constant practice of the elder people. But, it is urged, we have had wars with the Senones. Have the Volscians, have the Æquians never engaged us in battle? It is true, our capital has been taken by the Gauls; but by the Tuscans we have been forced to give hostages, and by the Samnites to pass under the yoke. However, upon a review of all our wars, none will be found to have been more speedily concluded than that with the Gauls, and from that time uninterrupted peace has existed. Identified with us in customs, in civil and military accomplishments, and domestic alliances, let them rather introduce among us their gold and wealth, than enjoy them without our participation. All the institutions, Conscript Fathers, which are now venerated as most ancient, were once new; the plebeian magistrates were later than the patricians, the Latin later than the plebeian; those of other nations in Italy came after the Latin; the present admission of the Gauls will also wax old, and what is this day supported by precedents will hereafter become a precedent." This speech was followed by a decree declaring the Æduans capable of a seat in the Senate.

The fall of the Roman Empire has been attributed to various causes, but, from a consideration of such facts as that here presented, I think there can be no doubt of the correctness of the conclusion mentioned (page 108), that it was due to extinction of the Roman ethnical element. The special Roman population so rapidly depreciated that the difficulty became incurable even by the most energetic legislation.

National policy, then, exercises a prodigious influence on population, though the particular form of government may have but little effect. It would not have been of the smallest consequence to England, in 1790, what her form of government might have been —republican, oligarchical, or monarchical; her mechanicians, Watt, Arkwright, Hargreaves, Crompton, Cartwright, by their inventions of the steam-engine, the spinning-frame, the jenny, the mule, the power-loom, the carding-machine, had put her in a position to monopolize the markets of the world. Industrial interests very quickly became paramount in the state. In fifty years she had not only doubled her population, but, as we have said, her machine power had become equal to thirty millions of men. In that period she almost quadrupled her wealth, notwithstanding losses through the most surprising political folly. The talent of her inventors more than counterbalanced the ignorance of her statesmen. Her commercial men, in conquering India, found a compensation for the loss of America. Her salvation was due to her merchants and machinists, not to her politicians and military men. These, had they not been counteracted, would inevitably have brought her to ruin; those, in spite of every disadvantage, gave her an intrinsic strength equal to that of the Roman empire at its maximum, when its population was one hundred and twenty millions.

How was it that industrial activity thus developed population? It provided for human support, and increased the demand for labor. Moreover, during that period there was a reduction of mortality by nearly one third.

The general principles involved in determining population have long been understood and are very simple. The natural instinct which leads to increase, and which is the most powerful of human passions, is of uniform intensity. Arising in the peculiarities of our organization, it can never be interfered with except by interfering with the organization, and hence, in its intrinsic force, is the same from age to age in the same nation. In different nations, compared together, it doubtless exists in different degrees, being dependent in this respect, as might be easily proved, on climate. In Western Europe we may estimate its value from this, that if there be a perfect freedom for its unrestrained action, and its results be submitted to no unusual causes of mortality, it will double a population in twenty-five years.

Such being the absolute value of the generative force of society, the observed result in any case depends on the resistances. A human being must be fed, clothed, and sheltered, conditions the procurement of which implies labor. Insufficient food, inadequate clothing, imperfect shelter, are the resisting forces in the problem of Population. Even with a free play for the generative force, the resistances control the effect, since they act in a double way—operating before birth so as in many instances to end life before that epoch, and after birth, insuring death by the starvation and misery they occasion. Practically speaking, then, it is quite true, as writers on Political Economy assert, that the increase of Population keeps pace with the increase of food. A critical examination will, however, satisfy us that this is only a statement of one particular case of the general problem, and that, philosophically, all the resistances ought to be included.

Since the time of the Jesuit Botero, it has been admitted that no legal encouragement to matrimony can be effective unless there is a corresponding increase of the means of subsistence. Modern statistics have established that in Europe there is a close connection between the number of marriages and the price of corn.

We must not overlook the interesting remark that the manner of operation of these Resistances is twofold—physical and intellectual. Cold, the want of food and of clothing, will act instantaneously in effecting a reduction. The history of every famine is an illustration of such abruptness; and the meagre population of countries in which the production of food is uniformly difficult, a testimony to the slower influence. But, besides this, man, being endowed with reason and continually looking to the future, puts a restraint upon himself. He will determine to refrain from marriage until he sees a clear prospect for the support of a family. He is unwilling to burden himself with a weight which he is not able yet to carry, and to inflict on those who must for many years be wholly helpless and dependent the inevitable consequences of distress and misery. In civilized, and especially in religious communities, this intellectual Resistance assumes very great power.

In any country the uniform generative social force goes on increasing the population until it is checked by the Resistances—the difficulty of feeding, clothing, sheltering—in short, by Poverty. It is a true maxim, that the principle of increase is always far more than sufficient to keep the population equal to its means of subsistence, and, indeed, in most countries, somewhat overpasses that point, and establishes a constant pressure on the limits of supply, and a certain amount of destitution is the inevitable consequence, there now being births that must be starved.

The statesman who is called upon to deal with the Problem of Population has, therefore, obviously the choice between two courses of action. He may touch the generative force, or he may touch the resistances; for though, as has been said, in an absolute sense the power is uniform, yet there exist means by a resort to which its consequences may be indirectly interfered with or rendered nugatory. It seems to me, however, that practice in this direction must always imply immorality, and that an enlightened man will rely exclusively on the other mode.

Would any one undertake to regulate the amount of air which shall be inspired in a given period of time, or the amount of food that shall be consumed? Would any one legislate as to the quantity of water that shall be lost by perspiration? We recognize in these various things the connection between organization and its result.

So in that other case, to which with needful obscurity I refer, he deceives himself who supposes that he can interrupt action while organization subsists: at the most, the effect is illusory, and is finding its manifestation in some other way. Public Celibacy is private wickedness. It is this dreadful truth, as applicable to communities, which has induced several European governments to enter on those methods against which every religious man must revolt—the organization of prostitution.

The other mode of influencing population we may consider without embarrassment. More food, cheaper clothing, better houses, are insured by increased remunerative labor, and this is instantly followed by increase of numbers. These also are things which fall within the scope of enlightened legislation. To these must be added those noble discoveries we owe to physicians, such as vaccination, improved methods for the cure of diseases, and measures for the abatement of pestilence. These, by securing to the productive laborer more vigorous health and by diminishing the death-rate, add directly and indirectly to the population. A similar result must occur from inventions which yield cheap clothing suited to the different seasons of the year, or add to the comforts and conveniences of houses.

From this superficial consideration of the Problem of Population we gather a most instructive lesson—the same that we have already learned from our inquiries respecting the origin, maintenance, distribution, and extinction of animals and plants. This lesson is, that the world is governed by Law. The generation of human life, the production of men, may be controlled by political agency and political conditions. Increases or diminutions of responsible immortal souls may be determined by statesmanship.

Under the influence of such natural laws Europe received its population from its Asiatic intruders. Climate and other exterior conditions separated it into nations, of which each thenceforth pursued its special way of life, imitating, as far as circumstances would permit, the successive stages of development of an individual.

There is a progress for races of men as well marked as is the career of one man. There are thoughts and actions appertaining to specific periods of life in the one case as in the other. The march of individual existence shadows forth the march of race existence, being, indeed, its representation on a little scale. Among humble animals intercommunication converts groups into an individual. The hive is moved by a common sentiment, the birds of passage are marshaled in a suitable array. Among men, speech and writing mould successive generations and different nations into one person. A society solicited by determinate physical influences would pass forward through a path as definite as that exhibited by a single man. A second society, completely separated from the preceding by space or by time, would, under like influences, do exactly the same thing. It is not a mere tendency, it is an actual performance. The infant of our time develops in the same way, and performs actions suitable to his stage, as did the infant a thousand years ago. He who is born in Asia advances through the same stages, exhibiting therein corresponding actions as he who is born in America. The variations we perceive, as our examination of these actions becomes more minute, arise from the disturbance of temporary and local causes, and the voluntary reaction of individuals on one another. No matter what diversity or dissimilarity we find at first, as we contemplate them with fixed attention and sufficiently long, their sameness becomes more and more manifest.

As in the Individual, so in the Nation, the time for psychical change corresponds with that for physical. In the individual, structural development is the harbinger of the display of new functions. Examined from the first moment of life throughout the ascending course, a variation in function is ever preceded by alteration in construction—so completely, indeed, that either being perceived, the other may be predicted. From this we gather the all-important conclusion that in national life it is altogether impossible to have advancement unless there be a corresponding material change. We vainly attempt the improvement of a race, intellectually or morally, by missionary exertion or by education, unless we simultaneously touch its actual physical condition. Any impression made upon that gives the possibility of accomplishing the other. The conclusion to which we thus arrive from purely physiological considerations is strengthened by actual experience. Does the splendid generosity of Christendom in behalf of the heathen world receive that fruit which is fairly its due? Are not the expected successes from year to year postponed?

The mental change which has occurred in Europe during the last two centuries was rendered possible by concurring material changes. Of what avail is education, except it be in presence of an ameliorated social condition? The diminution of the blue-eyed races on that continent shows how profound has been the physiological change; and better shelter, better clothing, better food, were the necessary precursors of better mental conceptions. Great amendments in the daily life of communities, great improvements in their manner of thinking, can only be attained by corresponding physical modifications.

It is with reluctance I acknowledge how small is the influence exerted by mere persuasion or even example. To elevate or to depress a group of men, it is necessary to touch their physical condition. If it were not so, how different would the career of the Indians upon this continent have been! With the illustrious example of the white race before their eyes, ought they not to have joined in the progress, co-partners with us in a glorious advance? How do those well-meaning men, who hope to accomplish the conversion and civilization of Nations by the preaching of a single missionary, account for the facts we have here? The white American and the red Indian, in presence of one another, offer the missionary problem in its grandest proportions. We turn away from the undeniable result with disappointment and pain.

A people who have occupied the same soil beyond the memory of man, and who have never been disturbed by admixture with others, may present a social condition of repose and stability—a tendency to persist in their habits, whatever those habits may be; if they are hunters and warriors, hunters and warriors they may continue. Conservatism is stamped upon them. They show no disposition to advance, and hence, no matter how active their intrinsic life, socially they are in repose. It is this state of stagnation which constitutes in European countries the real difficulty of elevating by education the lower orders. They cling to their maxims of life, no matter how evil—to their religious ideas, no matter how absurd, with a perversity that is almost beyond belief. At the best, they may be taught to imitate, but never to comprehend. They are at once impenetrable to knowledge and intolerant of change. The peasant, who cultivates his ancestral roods with the antique implement used in the Roman times, looks with a mixed sentiment of derision and abomination on an improved plow. His intellectual stagnation can not be overcome by any legislation, nor even by the force of example. Experience the most melancholy teaches us that the hand of violence can alone arouse him, the hand of violence alone improve him. It is this consideration which suggests to the philosophical mind a sad apology for the iniquities and calamities of conquest and war.

A people who are new to the climate in which they live—who have not attained a physiological correspondence with its conditions—who are incessantly, universally, and profoundly disturbed by foreign blood-admixture, will exhibit a scene of intense social activity. Among them will not be found that dead-weight of old communities, an obtuse lower class, almost impenetrable to knowledge and hating improvement; but, in all the social members, thought takes the direction of individual and general improvement. From the bosom of the mass emerge with more facility and more numerously those who are gifted with superior endowments, who in an old community disentangle themselves from obscurity with much difficulty, or perhaps not at all. Here there is nothing of stagnation; all is commotion and advance.

I do not propose here to consider in detail the complications that must have occurred in the advancing progress of European nations, through their interaction upon each other.

It is often affirmed that blood-admixture implies thought-variation. By this is meant that the intermingling of one race with another gives rise to a product not only participating in the bodily lineaments of its progenitors, but in the mental lineaments too. Incorporation with a base race will lower the standard of a superior one.

The historical instances that might be quoted in proof of this are very numerous. Selecting one as an illustration, since I have had occasion to refer to Egypt before, I may return to that case again. Its language proves to us that in pre-historic times that country was wrested from its original African owners by successful Asiatic invaders. The occurrence of words referable to Indo-Germanic roots establishes that fact. The consequences of this event are seen in the social organization. The existence of caste distinctions is an inevitable memento of violent conquest. The superior caste is the descendant of the conquering race. In Egypt there were castes.

But more than this, Religious ideas are indications of the social state. What is the interpretation that we must put on mummied bulls, and cats, and snakes? The adoration paid to them, was it the adoration of intelligent minds? The priesthood of Egypt retained in purity the monotheistic conceptions their ancestors brought from Asia, keeping them for the initiated; but the social condition of the nation required a base adulteration with the African worship of beasts.

The ruling class, whose conceptions are made manifest to us by the stupendous ruins and eternal architecture they have left, are then not to be blamed for the policy of exclusion they adopted. Their daily experience brought them in contact with too many tokens of the deterioration their race had suffered in the old times by blood-admixture. Instinctively they shut out the foreigner. They kept the Hebrew under his taskmaster apart; they would neither eat with him nor mix with him. They made it death for the European to set his foot in their country—that country of which, as they mournfully knew, the true emblem was a sphinx, with a human head and an animal body.

It is not consistent with the prosperity of a Nation to permit heterogeneous mixtures of races that are physiologically far apart. Their inferior product becomes a dead weight on the body politic. If Italy was for a thousand years after the extinction of the true Roman race a scene of anarchy, its hybrid inhabitants being unable to raise it from its degradation, how indescribably deplorable must the condition be where there has been a mortal adulteration with African blood.

At the close of the present century there will probably be ninety millions of white inhabitants in the United States, and only about nine millions of colored. The periodical oscillations the black population has exhibited — their increasing more rapidly during one decade, as from 1820 to 1830, and declining during another, as from 1830 to 1840—will probably be obliterated, if due, as is thought, to the excessive importation of African slaves from 1800 to 1808. In the slower increase of the colored population, as compared with the white, supposing no direct political action to be resorted to, lies the solution of the Negro problem in America.

The progress of blood-admixture is also very obvious. In 1850 one ninth of the colored class were returned as mulattoes, but in 1860 the proportion had risen to one eighth. Of every 100 colored births, 17 were mulattoes and 83 blacks. There is every reason to believe that the mingling of the two races is unfavorable to the vitality of their hybrid product.

Let us now, in conclusion, proceed to apply the philosophical facts we have been considering by the light of historical evidence to the special case of our own country.

The principles chiefly to be borne in mind are these—that the political effect of emigration depends upon the grade of society from which the emigrating mass has issued, being very different in the case of the laboring and of the intellectual classes respectively—that homogeneousness in a community imparts stability, though it eventually implies stagnation—that a community suffering incessant blood-disturbance will exhibit social activity, though, if the disturbing element is very base, a corresponding depreciation of its absolute value will ensue.

In the Southern States there are two races physiologically distinct—the white, which may be regarded as not liable to blood-contamination, and therefore becoming yearly more and more homogeneous; the black, liable, as we have seen, to increasing contamination of so extraneous and different a kind that the result becomes purposeless.

In the Northern States the blood-disturbance is through emigration. Its effect would be more marked if the stream did not flow mainly from Ireland and Germany, countries bounded by the same annual isothermals that limit New York on the north and Washington on the south. The movement which this class of population has to accomplish, to come into correspondence with the new conditions, is not great; but a careful observer will not fail to detect the retardation it impresses on the movement of its predecessors, and their corresponding detention in the lower intellectual states. The manner of thought of the whole community is less definite, its ideas less settled, its intentions less precise.

The Atlantic States have been the seat from which has issued the emigration destined to people the West. So far as their agricultural population is concerned, several of them may be regarded as having passed into a stationary condition. Of this, Vermont may be taken as an example, its census report for 1860 being substantially the same as that for 1850. If the limit of land-support has thus been reached, any farther advance must be looked for from commercial and manufacturing avocations. The Northwestern States offer a striking contrast. In the same decade Illinois doubled its population. Owing to their remarkable salubrity and unrivaled fertility, those regions are fast becoming the granary of Europe.

From the older states, in this manner, a very large portion of their population has been removed, in the general aggregate about one fourth having emigrated. In 1850 the large number of 4,176,000 whites were living in states where they were not born. In thirty states the native emigrants have chiefly preferred to locate in a state adjacent to that of their birth; the overflow has been greatest nearest its sources, yet progressive and diffusive in all directions. In general, and in obedience to the principle I have indicated, these emigrants move on parallels of latitude.

Now it is to be observed that the countries thus settled bear a resemblance, social and political, to those from which their population was first derived; a fact pointing to the conclusion that the abstraction made from the Atlantic States has been in a proportional manner from each of their three social grades. The effect of this has been to keep those states intellectually in a stationary condition, or to retard the development they would otherwise have made. Society, retaining in them more or less completely its interior primitive balance, has lost the advantage that would have been derived had the field of action been limited, the population more dense, the mental competition more violent. This is the explanation of the remark so often made, that our material prosperity and our mental progress have not advanced with an equal step.

The emigrating mass has also been placed under extraordinary conditions. Peopling an uninhabited region, it has suffered no deterioration from blood-admixture with lower tribes. The change that is being impressed upon it is altogether the effect of climate. Physically it hastens to come into correspondence with the new circumstances, and is ever moving in an ascending course. The length of time to be occupied in the metamorphosis before complete accordance is gained must be very considerable, and subject to a perpetual retardation, if continued emigration is all the time going on.

On the other hand, the length of time and the course to be gone through are shortened by that artificial equalization of Climate accomplished in civilized life. The building and warming of houses, the adjustment of clothing, the selection of food, compensate very largely for differences of climate, and bring us all to a more homogeneous state.

Of course, it would be in vain to deny that while all this is taking place, and as matters now stand, the intellectual position is very far below that which will inevitably be ultimately reached. Our journalism, our criticism, our educational establishments, bear evidence to the depression under which they necessarily labor. In fact, our situation is such that we actually can not profitably take advantage of the knowledge that we do possess.

An illustration will point out what I mean. A Virginia planter grows tobacco on his land until he has exhausted it. Of what avail to him is agricultural chemistry, with all its great discoveries? It might cost him five hundred dollars an acre to repair the mischief he has done to his estate; but he can buy virgin lands in the West at a dollar and a quarter an acre. Agricultural colleges are of no use to him. And so, for miles together in the Southern States, there are desolated and forsaken tracts—old fields, as they are called. But, if land is worth little, labor is worth much. Whoever can invent a labor-saving machine will make money. So our improvements are not in the direction of agricultural chemistry, but of agricultural mechanism.

In like manner with our educational establishments. Many intelligent persons speak depreciatingly of them, not considering duly the invisible pressure there is upon them. Their humble position for the time being is unavoidable. It is not to be amended by the system of multiplying them. That only makes them more importunate rivals in beggary. For years to come our public schools must be the seats of superficial learning; and we must accept it as an unavoidable fact, with the sad consequence taught us by European statistics, that that kind of instruction does not lead to the diminution, but rather to the increase of immorality. We must pass through the temporary evil to reach the final good.

Such I consider to be the present effect of the emigration that has been going on from the Atlantic States to the West—we endure a temporary retardation. But, should the course of that emigration be shortly diverted to the South, an event by no means beyond the bounds of possibility, the conditions of the problem are essentially altered, and far-seeing statesmen will discern that the experience we have hitherto had will be altogether inapplicable. The blood-admixture that must inevitably ensue with the white population of the South—a population that has nearly become homogeneous, nearly in agreement with the climate it is inhabiting, which has hitherto been disturbed by emigration to only an insignificant extent, and which, in its origin, was sensibly different from ours—that blood-admixture will make itself powerfully felt in the consequences that must ensue.

In these remarks as to the probability of an emigration to the South, it will doubtless be perceived that there is implied the transient nature of the existing alienation, an extinction of the bitterness of feeling pervading that portion of the country. There is a great difference between Civil and Foreign Wars as respects the permanence of the sentiments they engender. History is full of examples how speedily the feuds of a Civil War die away. Man is so constituted that he spontaneously resigns to oblivion his unsuccessful undertakings; and, since they form by far the larger proportion of the things he does, he is reconciled by habit to that forgetfulness. The vanquished in a civil strife avoids a recollection of his disappointed hopes. The victor abstains from a contemplation of his success: he feels that he can afford to forget even glory; and so the memory of such events speedily passes away. New objects, new motives, new pursuits are presented, and society starts again on a new basis. How brief a space it took, in the old times, to obliterate all memory of the awful civil wars of the Roman Empire—in later times, of those of England! It will take a still shorter period to do the same in the activity of human life in America.

The Pacific front of America, compared with its Atlantic front, presents differences so striking, that the future physiological effect can not fail to be important. "A cold sea-current so reduces the temperature of summer, that July is only eight or nine Fahrenheit degrees warmer than January, and September is the hottest month. For this reason, Indian corn fails to come to maturity, though wheat and other cereals, as well as orchard fruits, attain their utmost perfection. The elastic atmosphere and bracing ef fect of the climate have been remarked by settlers from all parts of the world."

From the remarks made on page 91, it will be inferred that the Pacific shore of the United States is destined hereafter to be the scene of an active Asiatic emigration. So vast is the mineral and agricultural wealth of those regions, so importunate the demand for labor, so remunerative its result, that the settled and torpid populations of China, Japan, India, can not fail to be affected. Already from the first of those countries the vanguard of such an intruding column has appeared. The Chinese population of California is far from insignificant, and is steadily increasing: in 1860 it was 34,933. It is of no importance that for the present these people look upon the country they thus visit as merely a temporary abode, in which money is to be made, and that, as their moderate expectations of a competency are fulfilled, they hasten to return to their native place. That is the natural timidity of early adventurers.

But these, in due season, will be followed by others having more settled intentions. The dislike the American population has to them once abating—that temporary dislike which all races of men who differ in aspect, in ideas, in religion from one another always entertain—the general principles of the system of the Republic will come into powerful effect. The facility for acquiring proprietorship in land, the certainty of its tenure, are temptations that no laboring class can resist. In the same street will be seen the Joss-house, the Synagogue, the Mosque, the Chapel, the Church.

Considering that, under the circumstances of the case, the individuals who are thus destined to disturb the Pacific Coast must necessarily issue from the lower social grades of the countries from which they come, their admixture with the native American population can not be viewed without anxiety. The Pacific States will do well to look to their public schools, laying broad and munificent foundations for their educational system, giving no encouragement to the use of any foreign tongue, and fusing into their mass, as thoroughly and rapidly as may be, their inevitable hybrid population.

With Eastern blood will necessarily come Eastern thoughts, and the attempt at Eastern social habits. I have already (page 113) referred to the political power of polygamic institutions. It must not be forgotten that they are in accordance with the sentiments of Asiatics. Especially, also, should it be borne in mind that they have already obtained a firm root in Utah. There is imminent danger of the spread of those institutions in the West. As men approach the confines of Asia, they seem to be affected by its moral atmosphere.

Nor should we overlook an additional source of disturbance from the population of Mexico—a base, a hybrid population. Whatever may be the political destiny of that country, contamination from it is unavoidable. The day will come when the sentiments expressed by the Emperor Claudius in relation to the Gauls, which I have quoted, page 149, will be urged in the Senate of the United States in relation to these people.

For the sake of drawing my reader's attention forcibly to this prospective state of affairs on the western front of the Republic, I have dwelt in some detail on the history of Arabian conquests and their extraordinary permanence. If he should see this interesting subject in the same light that it presents itself to me, I would ask his perusal of Chapters XI. and XVI. of my "History of the Intellectual Development of Europe."

Whatever may at present be the strength of the sentiment of disapproval or even of detestation with which we regard polygamy, we can not conceal from ourselves the strong temptations that will arise for its adoption in the West. We should remember how easily and how often, in an evil hour, great and even religious communities may be led astray. Our present abhorrence of this vice is no greater than was the abhorrence of human slavery in England a few years ago. Yet, because of a contingent political advantage—the division and consequent neutralization of a maritime rival—that country forgot her noblest philanthropic traditions, and arrayed herself in moral support of the slave power in America.

Warned by such a conspicuous example, we need not be surprised if hereafter there should be politicians—statesmen I will not call them—who may see in an extension of the practices of Utah a solution of the portentous problem of the admixture of the Pacific races. As the Saracens Arabized the north of Africa in the course of a very few years, they may believe that it is possible to Americanize those races.

Fifty years ago it would have been thought incredible that a polygamic state should exist in the midst of Christian communities of European descent; and yet a community, whose foundation rests on a religious imposture, has carried before our eyes that institution into practical effect, and is fast becoming rich and powerful.

There is always a probability of the public adoption of political ideas when they concur with the interests or passions of those to whom they are addressed; and conversely, it is from a want of such a concordance that attempts at reformation and elevation of the ideas of men so often prove failures. We can not deny the melancholy fact that men are guided much less by their own perceptions of right and wrong than by an apprehension of what public opinion in the case may be. Many will brave their own conscience — few society. Conscience may be mystified and blunted, but over society an individual has very little control. Hence it comes to pass that personal morality is too often much more the consequence of public opinion than of individual conscience; and hence the explanation of the remark so often made by observant persons, that men who are knaves as individuals, may yet, as a community, be honest.

This lax morality may, I believe, be more conspicuously detected among trading communities than among agriculturists. Life among the latter is individually more independent, but position in the former turns altogether on the consideration and credit that a man enjoys among those with whom he has dealings. He is constrained to comport himself according to their standard.

Where public opinion has been dexterously manufactured, and the interests and passions of men are insidiously provoked, very serious political faults may be perpetrated. No community can be altogether safe from such risks.

Since the decline of the Roman Empire, no nation has been called upon to deal with questions of civil policy so extensive and profound as those that must necessarily occupy the attention of the Republic. In Europe, the nations that have risen to what is there considered to be imposing power occupy comparatively small geographical surfaces; the problems in which they are interested have not the grandeur assumed by analogous problems here. With them, for instance, the effect of climate is but small, the consequences of emigration easily foreseen. Though those nations may assume very striking importance as regards the distribution of wealth, they sink at once into insignificance as respects its creation. There is nothing in Europe that answers to the vast deposits of metals and minerals in North America—nothing to its cotton, its tobacco—nothing to the agriculture of the prairies. The whole population of that continent could be settled in the Mississippi Valley, and find itself all the better for the change.

Still more, those nations are fettered by the results of the policy of past ages. They perpetually find stumbling-blocks in their way that are moss-covered and rotten, yet sufficiently impracticable to arrest their advancement completely. With the noblest aspirations, what can Italy do in presence of the anachronism of Rome? In France it is not the arbitrary will of the sovereign, but the public necessity that denies free speech and a free press.

But Europe never possessed that inappreciable privilege that has fallen to the lot of America—unity.

The intentions of her greatest and best men are thwarted by the impossibility of securing consistent actions among so many rival and antagonistic states. It is because of her want of it that, after so many centuries of trial, she has attained to no settled maxims of political life, and to no definite religious opinions.

Whatever, therefore, can make firm the bond of union on this continent, will aid in securing development of national power. An inflexible resolution, in the midst of the unparalleled sacrifices of the civil war, has shown how thoroughly that principle is appreciated. Was ever such a thing known in the world before as the spending of eight hundred millions of dollars a year, for four successive years, to sustain an idea? That fact betokens the future grandeur of the Great Republic! Climate and Emigration may tend to divide; but as long as that principle is so steadfastly kept in view and so irresistibly maintained, the means will certainly be found to neutralize their prejudicial effects.

# CHAPTER III.

## ON THE POLITICAL FORCE OF IDEAS.

*Ideas act on masses of men in a double manner, sometimes exerting an impelling, sometimes a resisting agency.*

*The Impelling power of Ideas is illustrated in the case of Mohammedanism, of which the political development as attained in Spain, and the Intellectual, as manifested in the philosophy of Averroes, are described.*

*The Resisting power of Ideas is illustrated in the case of the Jews. A brief sketch is given of their history, their sacred writings, and the modifications impressed upon them by the Persians, Greeks, and Arabs. It is their Messianic idea that resists the influences of Conquest and Time, and preserves them a separate people among all nations.*

*Man may comprehend Nature and subjugate physical forces. Under this Idea modern civilization is advancing. It is illustrated by a sketch of certain scientific discoveries and useful inventions.*

*The ecclesiastical causes of the European opposition to Science are explained, and the duty of America to develop and protect free thought is enforced.*

PHILOSOPHICAL conceptions of the historical progress of humanity must not be altogether of a material kind. Thus far, however, such has been the view offered in the preceding pages, which have been occupied with a consideration of the control of Climate over the constitution of man, and the Effects of Emigration. To this we have now to add the impelling and resisting power of Ideas. Ideas force humanity forward, though Nature has prepared the path along which the course must be run. They also furnish a bulwark that can resist the attacks of Time.

An Idea may therefore possess supreme political influence. A sentiment expressed by a few words may break up nationalities venerable for their antiquity, rearrange races of men, and revolutionize the world.

Many instances present themselves as suitable illustrations of these truths. Rome, for example, would yield an appropriate text. I turn, however, from cases which perhaps might lose their weight because of our familiarity with them, to one which, partly from prejudice and partly from policy, has hitherto been very much sequestered from our view.

On the eastern shore of the Red Sea, a fringe of fertile land received from the people of antiquity the designation of Arabia the Fortunate, or Happy. This Paradise, described as a land of incense and perfumes, recedes through low ranges of interior hills, and loses itself in endless deserts of sand. Of its mountains, some, as Horeb and Sinai, have become sanctified in the history of the human race. In the dry season scarce ever a cloud is seen on the sky. It is a riverless country, but in the rainy season the gorges contain rushing torrents. In different localities the temperature greatly varies: there are nights that are freezing cold, and days when the heat rises to 100°.

Here and there, embosomed in the sand, are beautiful oases, like those of Africa, natural gardens of wonderful luxuriance in the midst of a frightful sterility. The hot breath of the simoom that blows over the sultry waste feels as though it issued from the mouth of a furnace. The moving and bending columns that seem to reach to the sky, into which eddying whirlwinds work up the shifting sands, are said, in the poetical imagery of the inhabitants, to conceal beneath their dusty veil fleeting genii of the desert, angels of desolation, bowing their heads in homage to the Lord.

A paradise it was truly called. See of what valuable products it is the native home—the sugar-cane, the banana, the tamarind, the cotton-tree, the nutmeg, and the melon in all its varieties. Here flourish the date-tree, the cocoa, the fan-leaved palm, the fig, orange, vine, quince, apricot, almond, and plantain. The horticulturist may envy its botany; the physician bestow a nod of approval on a land that has given him the castor-oil plant and senna, and brought him many a profitable fee.

How much has the morality of the world been improved by coffee, first brought from Arabia! A substitute for intoxicating drinks, it has refined society, imparted innocent comfort to individuals, and peace to many a family. We abuse the abstemious religion of Mecca, the berry of Mocha we use.

The wilderness of Arabia is the birthplace of that most noble of all quadrupeds, the horse. Though his neck is clothed with thunder, and the glory of his nostrils is terrible—though he paweth in the valley and rejoiceth in his strength—though he swalloweth the ground in his fierceness and rage, neither can he persuade himself that it is the sound of the trumpet—though he smelleth the battle afar off, the thunder of the captains and the shouting, he plays with the Bedouin children that are round his master's tent. How deeply has a love of that beautiful creature affected the civilization of Europe! What had it not to do with chivalry! It turned the bloodthirsty warrior into a gentle and courteous knight.

If, as we have seen, Climate and the aspect of Nature give a special character to humanity, what kind of men should we expect in a riverless and forestless country—the companions of the camel and the horse? With a just pride, the inhabitants boast that their land has been the birthplace of the sciences and of the religion of half the human race.

In the year 569 was born at Mecca, a little town in that country, now sacred in the eyes of all Mussulmen, a man who has exerted an enduring influence on the human race—Mohammed, by Europeans surnamed the Impostor. Though descended from an ancient and proud family, his early life was spent in penury; and while only yet a boy of thirteen years, he was constrained so completely to give himself up to the pursuits of trade, that his enemies have affirmed he never knew how to read or write. Industry, and marriage with an opulent widow, whose agent he had been for a length of time, gave him wealth at last, and enabled him, before he had reached forty, to abandon his mercantile pursuits.

In very remote times—so remote that the circumstance had almost degenerated into a legend—there had fallen at Mecca, from the sky, a mass of iron, such as is now termed a meteoric stone. The primitive inhabitants had guarded this celestial body with religious care, erected a temple for its custody, and worshiped it as a god. Their idolatry had also extended to the adoration of certain graven forms.

Whether through the self-denial of a too abstemious life, or through that profound religious melancholy into which good men who have had large experience of the vanities of the world sometimes fall, Mohammed became the victim of mental illusion. There were unseen voices that whispered to him, and phantoms that he saw. In lucid intervals he suspected the evil into which he was falling, and warned his wife Chadizah that he feared he might become insane.

From the Jewish anchorets who of old sought a retreat beneath the shade of the palms of Engaddi, who beguiled their weary hours in the chanting of psalms by the bitter waters of the Dead Sea—from the philosophic Hindoo, who sought for happiness in bodily inaction and mental exercise, to the preaching soldier, who enforces his opinions by the edge of his sword, the stages of delusion are numerous and successive. But, so far from being impostures, these are nothing more than may be produced at any time. In the brain of man, impressions of whatever he has seen or heard, of whatever has been made manifest to him by his other senses, nay, even the vestiges of his former thoughts, are stored up. These traces are most vivid at first, but by degrees they decline in force, though they probably never completely die out. During our waking hours, while we are perpetually receiving new impressions from things that surround us, such vestiges are overpowered, and can not attract the attention of the mind; but in the period of sleep, when external influences cease, they emerge from oblivion, and the mind, submitting to the delusion, groups them into the fantastic forms of dreams. By the use of opium and other drugs which can blunt our sensibility to passing events, these phantasms may be evoked. They also offer themselves in the delirium of fevers and in the hour of death.

It is immaterial in what manner or by what agency our susceptibility to the impressions of surrounding objects is benumbed, whether by drugs, or sleep, or disease; as soon as their force is no greater than that of forms already registered in the brain, these last will appear before us, and deceptions and apparitions are the result. No man can submit to long-continued and rigorous fasting without becoming the subject of these hallucinations; and the more he enfeebles his organs of sense, the more vivid is the exhibition, the more profound the illusion.

The images that may thus emerge in the brain have been classed by physiologists among the phenomena of inverse vision or cerebral sight. From the moral effect to which they can give rise, we are very liable to connect them with the supernatural. In truth, they are, however, the natural result of the action of the nervous mechanism, which of necessity produces them when in the proper condition. It can act either directly, as in ordinary vision, or inversely, as in cerebral sight, and in this respect resembles those instruments which equally yield a musical sound whether the air is blown through them or drawn in. Yet, natural as their production is, such is the constitution of man, that the bravest and wisest encounter these fictions of their own imagination with awe. Few things, in fact, have exerted a greater influence on the career of the human race than these spiritual visitations. The visions of Mohammed have ended in tincturing the daily life of half the people of Asia and Africa for a thousand years. A spectre that came into the camp at Sardis unnerved the heart of Brutus, and thereby put an end to the political system that had made the great republic the arbitress of the world.

It is the localization of the phantom—that creation of the brain—among the bodies and things around us, that gives force to these illusions. The form of a cloud no bigger than the hand is perhaps first seen floating over the carpet; but this, as the eye follows it, takes on a definite shape, and the sufferer sees with dismay a moping raven perched on some of the distant articles of furniture. Or, out of an indistinct cloud, female faces, sometimes of surprising loveliness, emerge, a new face succeeding as a former dies away. The mind, ever ready to practice imposture upon itself, will at last accompany the illusion with grotesque or dreadful inventions. A sarcophagus, painted after the manner of the Egyptians, distresses the visionary with the rolling of its eyes. Sometimes, instead of a solitary phantom intruding itself among recognized realities, as the shade of a deceased friend opens the door and noiselessly steps in, the complicated scenes of a true drama are displayed—the brain becomes, as it were, a theatre. According as the travel or the reading of the sick man may have been, the illusion takes a style—black vistas of Oriental architecture that stretch away into infinite night—temples, and fanes, and the battlemented walls of cities, colossal Pharaohs sitting in everlasting silence with their hands upon their knees. "I saw," says De Quincey, in his Confessions of an Opium Eater, "as I lay awake in bed, vast processions that passed along in mournful pomp; friezes of never-ending stories, that to my feelings were as sad and solemn as if they were stories drawn from times before Œdipus or Priam, before Tyre, before Memphis. And, at the same time, a corresponding change took place in my dreams; a theatre seemed suddenly opened and lighted up within my brain, which presented nightly spectacles of more than earthly splendor."

Mohammed, having retired to the solitude of the desert, devoted himself to meditation, fasting, prayer, and became the victim of these cerebral delusions. He was visited by supernatural appearances, mysterious voices accosting him as the Prophet of God. It is related that, as he sat alone with Chadizah his wife, a shadow entered the tent. "Dost thou see aught?" said Chadizah, who remarked his agitation, and who, after the manner of Arabian matrons, wore her veil. "I do," said the Prophet; whereupon she uncovered her face and said, "Dost thou see it now?" "I do not." "Glad tidings to thee, O Mohammed!" exclaimed Chadizah; "it is an angel, for he has respected my unveiled face; an evil spirit would not." As his disease advanced, these spectres became more frequent. It was from one of them that he received the divine commission to preach. "I," said his wife, "will be thy first believer," and they knelt down in prayer together. Since that eventful night nine thousand millions of human beings have acknowledged him to be a prophet of God.

A preaching soldier! The qualities implied in that character belong only to the highest rank of men. Of such was Mohammed. His theology was simple —"There is but one God;" but to that he also added, "and Mohammed is his Prophet."

The great earthquake of Lisbon, in 1755, was felt from Norway to Morocco, from Poland to the West Indies. It absolutely lifted the whole bed of the North Atlantic Ocean. What a vast physical impulse that implies!

But is there no political force in an Idea? The dogma of Mohammed sent a quivering thrill through the souls of men from the Gulf of Guinea to the Chinese Sea. Three continents—Asia, Africa, Europe—rocked to their foundations under it. Empires venerable for their antiquity, religions covered with the hoar of antiquity, vanished away. As the breath can melt the graceful ice-forms that incrust a window on a winter's morning, so the breath of the Prophet melted away whole races of men and their works.

There is something wonderful in this propagation of thought from man to man. As a candle may be lighted from a flame, and again and again others may be kindled in succession one from another without any impairment of the intrinsic brightness, so thought passes from one to another, ever growing, never losing its innate force. That thought—the oneness of God, and a divine mission imposed on a man—passed forth from the Prophet and was received by his trusting wife. In the departing twilight of an Arabian summer's evening they knelt down, hand in hand, at the entrance of their tent. They prayed to the All-merciful that he would take pity on them and show them what to do. In a few months the fire had kindled in a few zealous disciples. It occasioned a brief struggle in Arabia: there were battles. God gave victory to his servant: the country bowed under the convincing argument of his sword. Within twelve years after the death of their great leader his followers had reduced the chief fortified places in Persia, Syria, Africa. They quickly extended their dominion a thousand miles east and a thousand west. The churches of Syria and of Asia Minor, that garden of the world, were utterly destroyed; above all, Jerusalem, the Holy City of the East, with all its touching recollections, was seized. In Persia, its native place, Magianism, a religion venerable for its antiquity, went down before the storm; in India, Vedaism, the worship of Nature, the pantheistic belief of one hundred and twenty millions of men, met its rival and master; in China, Buddhism, the settled creed of four hundred millions, shared the same fate. The tempest of Saracen armies pushed its conquering career along the north coast of Africa. Confronted by the impassable Atlantic, the Arabs turned aside into Spain, and held that country for as long as it is from the Norman conquest of England to our day. Almost as if by a miracle, the rest of Europe escaped.

"There is but one God, and Mohammed is his Prophet." The vanquished must make his choice between that confession, or tribute, or death.

Is there, then, no political force in an Idea? Gold and silver, and iron and coal, and cotton and oil, material things that are forced out of the earth, are these the divinities? An idea can shake humanity to its foundations, an idea can govern the world.

It is impossible to compress into the limited space at my disposal the long story of the consequences of all these wonderful political events. It is needful to make a selection, and I choose that which has proved to be the most closely connected with the history of Western Europe, and therefore with our own—the Saracen conquest of Spain.

Scarcely had the Arabs become firmly settled in Spain before they commenced a brilliant career. Adopting what had now become the established policy of the Commanders of the Faithful, the Khalifs of Cordova distinguished themselves as patrons of learning, and set an example of refinement strongly contrasting with the condition of the native European princes. Cordova, under their administration, boasted of more than 200,000 houses and more than a million of inhabitants. After sunset a man might walk through it in a straight line for ten miles by the light of the public lamps: seven hundred years after this time there was not so much as one public lamp in London. Its streets were solidly paved: in Paris, centuries subsequently, whoever stepped over his threshold on a rainy day, stepped up to his ankles in mud. The Spanish Mohammedans had brought with them all the luxuries of Asia. Their residences stood forth against the clear blue sky, or were embosomed in woods. They had polished marble balconies overhanging orange gardens, courts with cascades of water, retiring-rooms vaulted with stained glass speckled with gold; the floors and walls were of exquisite mosaics. Here a fountain of quicksilver shot up in a glistening spray, the glittering particles falling with a tranquil sound like fairy bells; there, apartments into which cool air was drawn in summer from flower-gardens. Clusters of frail marble columns surprised the beholder with the vast weights they bore. In the boudoirs of the Sultanas they were sometimes of verd antique, and incrusted with lapis-lazuli. Through pipes of metal, water both warm and cold, to suit the season of the year, ran into baths of marble; in niches, where the current of air could be artificially directed, hung dripping alcarazzas. There were whispering-galleries for the amusement of the women, labyrinths and marble play-courts for the children, for the master himself grand libraries. At this brilliant focus barbarian Europe lighted its lamp of civilization.

Such were the Khalifs of the West; such their splendor, their luxury. Considering the enchanting country over which they ruled, it was not without reason that they caused to be engraven on the public seal, "The servant of the Most Merciful rests contented in the decrees of God." What more, indeed, could they have had? But, considering also the evil end of all this happiness and pomp, we may well appreciate the solemn truth which these monarchs, in their day of pride and power, grandly wrote in the beautiful mosaics on their palace walls—an ever-recurring monition to him who owes dominion to the sword—"There is no conqueror but God."

From these political events I turn to philosophical results, with a view of showing what, in that direction, were the consequences of the fundamental Arabian idea.

History conspicuously teaches that there will always emerge from every great religious confession men who endeavor to cast light on its principles by the aid of human reason—men who will philosophize. If, therefore, we desire to measure the force of an idea and to master all its bearings intelligently, we must add to the estimate of its material or political momentum an appreciation of its philosophical development. That is what I now proceed to do in the present case.

Within a century after Mohammed's death, so active was the mental movement among his followers that they began to dispute about free-will and predestination. Soon in Bagdad controversies arose respecting the attributes of God, and philosophical schools were founded, the branches of which ramified along the coast of Africa into Spain, and in the opposite direction extended into the far East. We comprehend at once the spirit of these schools when we consider the bearing of the maxim of one destined eventually to stand at the head of all the rest· "The special religion of philosophers is to study what is sublime, and the most sublime worship that can be rendered to God is the study of his works." There, if I mistake not, was the secret of the Saracen delight in the cultivation of natural science.

At the capture of Alexandria, in the early days of Mohammedanism, the Saracens were brought in contact with the vestiges of Greek philosophy. The Christians whom they found there had long leaned to the views of Plato, whose doctrines had been cultivated by some of them with singular effect. On the other hand, the Saracens attached themselves to Aristotle as their scientific guide. And thus it came to pass that the higher aspects of Mohammedanism were tinctured with the opinions of that great Greek writer, and the Arabians held to be the expounders of the Aristotelian philosophy. A very great modern critic regards the attitude in which their philosophical schools stood as being a reaction against Arabism; but with diffidence I express an opposite opinion, believing that the doctrines maintained by them were the necessary extension of the fundamental dogma of their faith, that there is but one God.

That extension of their dogma was destined to shake Europe to its centre. Asserting the omnipresence of God, they affirmed that all human souls had emanated from him, and were destined to return ultimately to him, as a drop of water vaporized from the sea, though it may pass through a thousand vicissitudes, is pressed by an inevitable destiny, and sooner or later returns to the sea again. They developed these ideas into a vast system, distinguished by the vigor of its conceptions and the acuteness of its reasoning. It is needless to particularize the details of that system. Its general tendency may be gathered from a few of its doctrines and sentiments.

From the cardinal idea of Mohammedanism they therefore affirmed that the important doctrine of the Indestructibility and Conservation of Force, and its necessary consequence, the Unity of human souls, arose. They were the authors of the so-called modern theory of development, anticipating the most re-

N

cent writers on that subject in many of its details. Carrying the Fatalism of their creed into their philosophy—and it is such incidents as these that persuade me that they were not in antagonism to Arabism—they first give expression to that portentous maxim, "What can be, is." The adoption of such opinions bore, of course, at once on the great truth of the final accountability of man, making him an unresisting agent. In a scientific point of view that maxim was carried out to its consequences, as against the doctrine known as that of final causes. In the luxurious and splendid society of Spain such sentiments met a ready acceptance. Listen to what one of their most powerful writers says: he is co-ordinating the grand views of Aristotle on the world of living things, with the Fatalism of Mohammed: "There is an eternal sea of Being, on the surface of which play the oscillating and variable ripples of individuality. God deals with the general laws of the universe, not with individuals. He recognizes the ocean, not its waves." Interpreting the abstract doctrines of Aristotle by the light of their natural faith, they were thus brought at once to the self-indulgence of Epicurus and the doubt of Pyrrho. They said, "Permit all things, believe nothing." They professed that their conception of a perfect civil state is merely this: "It is that which requires neither a physician nor a judge."

These statements may convey an idea of the condition to which philosophy had come, not only among the Spanish Arabs, but also among those of Asia. The real birthplace of these opinions was Bagdad. From thence they ramified over all the Mohammedan world. Of their writers, the most celebrated was Averroes. Let us now see what were the consequences of these things in Europe.

It was during the pontificate of Innocent III., about the year 1200, that the Mendicant orders were established in the Roman Church. The course of ages had brought an unintelligibility into public worship. Latin, like an old dialect, had become obsolete; the modern languages were forming. Among those classes, daily increasing in numbers, whose minds were awakening, an earnest desire for instruction was arising. Multitudes were crowding to hear philosophical discourses in the universities, and heresy was spreading very fast. But it was far from being confined to the intelligent. The lower orders furnished heretics and fanatics too. To antagonize the labors of these zealots, who, if they had been permitted to go on unchecked, would quickly have disseminated their doctrines through all classes of society, the Dominican and Franciscan orders were founded. They were well adapted to their duty. It was their business to move among the people, preaching to them in their own tongue wherever an audience could be collected.

A very few years were needed to change totally

the aspect of the mendicant orders. No longer rope-bound, starving zealots, they became the most learned men in Europe, filling the chief professorships in the universities. They plunged deeply into the mysteries of Averroism, and were soon divided into parties. The Dominicans were animated with the fiercest hatred against the Arabs, denouncing them as infidel Epicureans; the Franciscans took the opposite side, and holding, for the time, control of the University of Paris, made it a focus of Averroism. It would be in vain to attempt to give an adequate conception of the scholastic disputations that arose. Wherever there was a monastery, there was a furious debate. Italy quickly became involved. Commercial prosperity had concentrated in Venice immense wealth. She had a powerful aristocratic class, and in that high society, as it had been in the high society of Spain, Averroism became fashionable. It held fast its ground all through the north of Italy. In a letter from Columbus, dated Hayti, October, 1498, he says: "Averroes is one of the writers who has made me divine the existence of the New World." That remark assures us that, in common with the progressive men of his time, the Great Admiral was familiar with the views of the Spanish Mohammedan. They were now beginning to produce important physical results, and preparing the way for that scientific school soon to be made glorious by the discoveries of Galileo, Torricelli, and the Florentines. The proud fabric of modern science, the prodigies of modern industry, our vast manufactures, came from this source.

In vain the Roman authorities, appreciating the whole state of the case, forbade the reading of the physical works of Aristotle in the University of Paris. The contagion broke out nearer home in the University of Padua, stimulated and sustained by the wealthy people of Venice. It was clear that strenuous measures must be resorted to to abate the trouble. The Papal government took its course, and by the Lateran Council, under Leo X., the formal condemnation of the philosophy of Averroes was pronounced.

But whoever is familiar with the writings of the Italian statesmen will trace to this source the maxims of policy indicated by them; and those maxims, spreading from Italy, where they had long been in use, became the secret principles of diplomacy all over Europe. It is only in much more recent times that they have been supplanted by purer and more honorable means.

Such is the progress, and such, often, the power of an Idea. From the mind in which it first originated it may spread, until at last, physically and intellectually, whole continents may be involved. It is useless, then, to say that ideas have no force. In truth, they govern the world. A tide of human intelligence followed the movement of the Arabian Crescent as a watery tide in the sea follows the motion of the moon. It may be that some of the results in the particular instance we have been considering are of a kind to meet our disapproval; but it is with their force, not with their goodness or evil, that we are concerned.

See how that dogma which obtruded itself on the disturbed fancy of an enthusiastic Arab in his tent, and haunted him like something supernatural—a dogma in part consisting of an everlasting truth known from the old times, and in part of a fiction never heard of before—gradually forced its way, overthrowing empires and remodeling societies! Think not that it made its way by the aid of the sword alone. The sword may for a moment change an acknowledged national creed, but it can not affect the consciences of men. Profound though its argument be, something far more profound is demanded to produce results such as have been occupying our attention.

The idea was suitable to the times, and to the condition of those to whom it was addressed. There lay the secret of its rapid spread—its intrinsic force on one hand, opportunity on the other.

Arabian history thus gives a most striking instance of the *impelling* power of an Idea. No better example of the *resisting* power of an Idea can be furnished than that afforded by Israelitish history. Ideas have a passive as well as an active political force.

What is it that, after more than twenty centuries of conquest, subjugation, and persecution—after exposure to all the allurements of idolatry and all the fascinations of philosophy—after transportation to every country under the sun—what is it that has kept this Asiatic people an undestroyed nation? Their idea of a Messiah or a Deliverer.

In the earlier periods of their history the Jewish people had continually shown a disposition to fall into the idolatries of the surrounding nations. Even under the eyes of their lawgiver they resumed in the desert the adoration of Apis, which they had learned in Egypt, and animal worship is but a step removed from Fetichism. The Syrian tribes among whom they were subsequently thrown had already passed to the more elevated form of star-worship, Baal and the crescent-horned Astarte, the sun and the moon, being their principal divinities. It was with difficulty that the rulers and prophets of Israel reclaimed them from their perpetual backslidings to these idolatries.

So long as the Jews maintained themselves as a compact and independent nation, these idolatrous lapses can only be regarded as transient maladies from which they easily recovered. But very different was it after the conquest of Jerusalem by Nebuchadnezzar and the carrying of the people into captivity. To the multitude, who had ever shown a disposition to adopt the idea of the corporealization of

God, and who had estimated the weakness or power of cities in warfare with their enemies by the weakness or power of their tutelary deities rather than by their military resources, the ruin of the Temple and the downfall of the Priesthood was a moral blow the force of which we can scarcely estimate. Their compulsory residence in Assyria established with that country connections and relationships which, so far from ending with the nominal restoration of the nation to its ancient seats, continued throughout their entire subsequent history, even after the final destruction of Jerusalem by the Romans. In Persia they learned Magianism. To that form of Religion, embraced, undoubtedly, the more readily because of the shock their own faith had sustained, we must impute all those novelties they exhibit after their return from captivity. Its philosophical aspect might even recommend it to the more intellectual among them. In one essential point it offered a correspondence to the Hebrew doctrine forbidding the worship of God under any graven image or form. Asserting the existence of one Great First Cause, it placed beneath him two subordinate powers, metaphorically set forth as Light and Darkness. It explained the co-existence of good and evil in the world on the principle that wherever there is brightness there must be shadow. It presented an impersonation of these powers in Ormusd, the Prince of Glory, and in Ahriman, or Satan, the embodiment of Evil or Darkness, beneath whom there were marshaled respectively armies of angels and dæmons. Originally Satan was created pure, but, becoming envious of the glory of Ormusd, he was precipitated into the abyss. Between these dual divinities an unceasing warfare was waged. And since the First Cause was far removed from all material things, incapable of being approached even by man, it was needful that there should be a mediator. Ormusd, the principle of benevolence and light, had created man in a state of purity and virtue; while Ahriman, the principle of evil and darkness, continually sought his destruction. In the last day of this conflict, when Ahriman is conquered and cast into darkness, the children of light who have been saved will enter into eternal glory. Not only is the soul of man immortal, but there is for the good a resurrection from the dead. The punishment of Ahriman is not, however, to be eternal: he will be purified in a Purgatory with torments of fire. The Magians admitted angelic influences under visible forms, and accepted the idea of Incarnation. They recognized the necessity of a tangible form of worship for the illiterate, and hence set forth, as emblems of Ormusd, Fire, Light, the Sun, to which devotions might be paid.

Magianism therefore presented a complete and consistent religious scheme very different from the fragmentary mythology of Europe, which offered no pervading idea. So far as its doctrine of a First Cause is concerned, it approached, as has been said, to the Israelitish conception. It dealt with the great moral problem of the existence of evil in the world. It had a Principle of Good and of Evil, a mechanism of Angels and Dæmons. It contemplated man as being exposed in this life continually to the wiles of the Devil. It included the idea of a Mediator between God and man; it asserted the immortality of the human soul, and a state of future rewards and punishments. Its ritual has descended to us in the "Zendavesta," or "Oracles of Life," said to be a revelation from Ormusd.

Before the Babylonian captivity the Jews seem to have entertained corporeal views of the nature of God, and not to have accepted the doctrine of a future life, but looked for rewards and punishments exclusively in this. They did not admit a resurrection from the Dead. But, after that event, many of the doctrines of the Magians are plainly to be seen in their religious belief; and, indeed, upon one of the more prominent of them, the great national schism between the Pharisees and Sadducees arose. The latter, assuming the air of an elevated philosophy, pretending to lift themselves above vulgar ideas, altogether rejected the articles of the existence of angels, the immortality of the soul, and of the future state. It has been the fortune of Magianism, on two occasions, to affect powerfully the Monotheism of the

West; once in thus completely modifying the Hebrew faith by imparting to it many new ideas, and again, in the early ages of Christianity, by amalgamating itself therewith, and giving origin to the varied forms of Gnosticism. Not only were Syria, Asia Minor, and Egypt filled with pseudo-Magian sects, but a permanent impression was imparted to the subsequent Catholic form. Of this, any one may be satisfied who compares the state of Christianity in the first century with that in the tenth, aiding himself in his examination by the acknowledged Magian creed. It is an interesting circumstance that the Catholic authorities charge the earlier Reformers with Magian tendencies under the forms of Manichæism. Thus the Albigenses, in the latter part of the twelfth century, the Waldenses, the Vaudois, the Picards, the Petrobrusians, are placed under that stigma.

The co-existence of conflicting ideas in the same religion may arise not only from conquest, when one caste is holding another in subjugation, but also in a society truly homogeneous, so far as origin is concerned, but which, in its progress, has become decomposed into two portions—a thinking class, and a class which is absorbed in the cares of supporting animal existence. With national development the number and influence of the first class steadily increases, and in the end it exercises a regulating political power. Such a society, therefore, will always exhibit a tendency to philosophical progress in its religious views; and if its condition is examined at intervals considerably apart, the advance that has been made is often very striking. Thus there can not be any doubt that among the ancient Israelites it was the current belief that Almighty God made his residence behind the veil of the Temple. In later times, when more noble and more worthy views of the divine nature were attained to, the same people could not possibly accept a doctrine expressing such a corporealization of God, and, with patriotic inconsistency, limited that occupancy to the time of the Temple of Solomon. Herein we see the effect of opinions originating in a more advanced class of society, and gradually ascended to by a lower. They end in producing compromises, the inconsistency of which is excused because of the necessities of the case.

Perhaps I may here be excused a passing remark on those venerable books constituting the Pentateuch, which not only serve as a guide to the daily life of Israel in all parts of the world, and are looked upon by Christendom with a sentiment of profound reverence, but which unhappily have been diverted from their original intent, and made to exert a most extraordinary, and, I will add, repressing influence on the advancement of scientific discovery.

I think that whoever will read this portion of the Holy Scriptures with critical care, having first brought his mind to a clear appreciation of the manners and opinions of the ancient Egyptians, and also of those of the Assyrians, will be forcibly drawn to the conclusion that the author, or rather authors of these books, lived nearer to the banks of the Euphrates than to those of the Nile. If such an expression may with propriety be used, their literary aspect is Assyrian, not Egyptian.

An author, even though inspired, must necessarily receive a tincture from the scenery, the time, the community in which he lives. The images and expressions he uses will all accord with a certain style. In literary composition, as in painting, there is a style which makes itself obviously manifest to the critical eye. Nay, even the handwriting of a man is readily detected by those who are familiar with it, though it would be very difficult for them to say wherein the peculiarity consists. I repeat it—the style of this portion of the Inspired Volume is Asiatic, not African.

For the sake of modern science, and of true religion too, it is deeply to be regretted that this interesting question can not be remitted to the state in which it was a century ago, when it was regarded, both by Christian and Jewish writers, as a point to be dealt with according to the rules of ordinary criticism, and not as a matter of sentiment.

With diffidence I would suggest that the treatment of this question will probably demand a renewed and critical examination of the authenticity of the fourteenth chapter of the second book of Esdras, called apocryphal. It is desirable to know what it was that determined so many very ancient and very great ecclesiastical writers — Irenæus, Tertullian, Clemens Alexandrinus, Basil, Jerome, Augustine, Chrysostom —to accept the affirmations of that chapter as true. They lived much nearer the date of these events than we do; perhaps they had more certain means to guide their judgment. They held that the original Pentateuch was lost or destroyed in the Babylonian captivity, and that the statement that Ezra is affirmed to make in the place above quoted must be received as accurate.

That statement is to this effect: that the original books were burnt; and that, for the purpose of furnishing a guide to the people, Ezra undertook to write all that had been done in the world from the beginning.

To this end, he took five amanuenses, and secluded himself for forty days. In that time the books were written; and the Most High ordered that the first portion of them should be published openly, that the worthy and the unworthy might read it.

But the latter portion was to be reserved for the wise, for in them is the vein of understanding, and the fountain of wisdom, and the river of knowledge. And Ezra did as he was ordered to do. There were, then, esoteric and exoteric books.

Ezra, a priest and Doctor of the Law, was a prisoner in Media in the reign of Artaxerxes I., king of Persia, B.C. 458. It may be added, to connect the recollection of these events with European chronology, that they happened about the time that Themistocles put himself to death.

To return from this digression: Persia imposed on the Jews an intellectual impression discoverable in all their subsequent history. It gave a special characteristic to their religious faith. Above all, on their return to their native country they brought with them the idea that has imparted to them, in subsequent ages, indestructibility. In their captivity they had been witnesses of many great political events. They had seen their Babylonian desolator made desolate, their victor vanquished. It was in the uncertainties and sufferings of these events, when they hung their harps on the willows and wept when they remembered Zion, that the hope of a Deliverer first arose; and in the greater calamities of after ages, this, which in the first instance was no more than a wished-for political event, became a fixed religious expectation. Experience had shown them that in the fall and rise of great empires they had been preserved. It taught them to look with an inflexible faith through all the vicissitudes of the future.

After the overthrow of the Persian Empire by Alexander the Great, the Jews were brought in con-

tact with a new intellectual disturbance—Greek philosophy. The Syrian Jews successfully resisted that influence; the trifling approaches made to it were of a very transitory kind. Such outward manifestations as the race-course and gymnasia, that had been established, did not suit the genius of Jerusalem. But it was far otherwise with those Israelitish emigrants who had settled in Egypt. Under the favoring climate of that country they became thoroughly Hellenized. Among them the philosophy of Plato found enthusiastic devotees, and through them the whole current of later European religious thought has been affected.

As they had withstood Greek, so, too, they withstood Roman influence. In vain Antiochus Epiphanes, who had long lived in Rome, tried to bring about a change; in vain succeeding princes renewed the attempt; the stubborn, stiff-necked people were as unyielding as adamant. The Pharisees, who constituted the patriotic party—Hebrews of the Hebrews—would have nothing to do with the fictions or philosophies of the West. They left that, with derision and detestation, to the infidel Sadducees.

Still again; when the Arabians overwhelmed by their military conquests Asia and Africa, though the Jew in one sense affiliated with the victorious intruder, in another, with an inborn instinct, he kept himself separate. The Syrian branch of the family, with its immovable austerities, had yielded in importance to the Egyptian: it had been more than decimated by the bitterness of Roman subjugation, both Pagan and Christian; but the Egyptian Israelite, though declining the forms of Mecca, gave his hand to the Saracen. They found a point of harmony in the great doctrine of the oneness of God. From this alliance both parties took benefit: the Arab gained philosophy, and the Jew political influence. Conjointly they forced upon Europe its chief modern characteristic—scientific advancement.

Not until the Syrian Jew had become modified by migrating to other countries did his character change. So long as he was in the chosen land, he was ever the same unyielding fanatic. He had no conception of art, either as expressed by painting or statuary. In possession of what he considered to be a supernatural revelation, it was impossible that literature should prosper with him, or even receive the smallest encouragement. His profound belief in signs and wonders was incompatible with science, and accordingly nothing deserving of that name existed in his nation.

But his mind as well as his sky changed when he migrated to other countries. He became great among the greatest in all these manifestations of the highest results of human civilization.

Scattered all over the world, Israel still, as a people, exists. Go where we will, we may always find its patriarchal graybeard, when all other earthly objects and pursuits are passing away, sitting in hourly expectation of an annunciation of the Messiah. It is that, and no miracle, which, through the wreck of nations and the extinction of men, has given to the Jew immortality. He lives through the force of an idea.

I can not close these remarks better than by quoting a passage of profound import from the learned author of the "Etudes d'Histoire Religieuse:"

"If, finally, we put to ourselves this question, Has Israel fulfilled its calling? has it, in the grand mingling of nations, kept the post that was originally intrusted to it? we reply without hesitation, Yes. Israel has been the stem on which the faith of the human race has been grafted. No people has taken its destiny so seriously as Israel; none has felt so vividly its joys and its sorrows as a nation; none has lived more thoroughly for an idea. Israel has vanquished Time, and made use of all its oppressors. The day when a false report caused us to celebrate one year too soon the taking of Sebastopol, an old Polish Jew, who spends his days in the Imperial Library, absorbed in reading the dusty manuscripts of his nation, greeted me with this quotation from Isaiah: 'Is it fallen, is it fallen, Babylon?' The victory of the Allies, as he saw it, was but the chastisement for violence practiced on his co-religionists by the man whom he called the Nebuchadnezzar and the Antiochus of our time. In that sad old man I seemed to see before me the living genius of that indestructible people. Over every ruin it has clapped its hands; persecuted by all men, on all men it has been avenged. For this it has needed but one quality—a quality which, however, man gives not to himself—endurance. It is by this that it has brought to pass the boldest predictions of its prophets. The world that despised it has come round to it. Jerusalem at this present hour is truly 'a house of prayer for all nations,' equally venerated by Jew, by Christian, by Mussulman."

These instances of the political force of Ideas in the case of the Arabians and the Israelites may serve as an introduction to the consideration of that grander idea under which modern civilization is evolving; it is, that man can comprehend Nature, and subjugate physical agents to his use.

A most audacious conception—the conquest of Nature! Like other grand ideas, it has slowly emerged from small beginnings and is steadily forcing its way. Resisted by influences that have gathered around them in the course of centuries political power, it has overthrown many and confronts the rest. Modern Europe is fast submitting herself to its rule.

It first formally appeared in the writings of Aristotle, and gained strength through the events consequent on the Asiatic campaign of Alexander the

Great. Under the auspices of the Ptolemies, who founded in Alexandria institutions for its encouragement, it received a marked development, and would probably have modified the aspect of human affairs, had it not been for the founding of the Byzantine Empire.

For it so fell out that the political position of Constantine the Great and his successors was incompatible with the protection of science, the knowledge of Nature. Those sovereigns placed themselves in inflexible opposition to it; and to the last, when they were overthrown by the Turks, used whatever power they had for its destruction. The policy they thus adopted became incorporated with the ecclesiastical system they represented, and, though with diminished force, it has descended to our times.

But it was not in Constantinople alone that events took this unhappy course. Papal Rome, through her ancient connection with the Byzantine policy, became in like manner committed; and her ecclesiastical influence, reaching even through the Reformation, still acts adversely on the investigation of Nature and against the free propagation of thought.

So far as Europe has found relief from this intellectual oppression, her deliverance has come through those people to whose history I have been referring —the Arabians and the Jews. Modern Science as well as modern Industry is their creation.

I now propose to devote a few pages to a partial illustration of what has been done toward obtaining a true knowledge of Nature, and the subjugation of physical agents to the use of man. But, though I were to increase by many times the space I can devote to this topic, I must necessarily leave it in a very imperfect, and therefore unsatisfactory condition. So vast is the body of information accumulated, that it exceeds the capacity of any one book, and transcends the understanding of any one man.

But, though imperfect in that respect, this sketch will be sufficient to give emphasis to the proposition I intend to rest upon it—that a Nation which is preparing itself for sovereignty among the powers of the earth must shake off the traditions of obsolete policy, and stand forth the defender and protector of free thought.

The process of attaining correct views of Nature has been marked by a continual decline of the mysterious and supernatural.

In the beginning of social as well as of individual life, the appearance of things is accepted as a reality. The blue concave of the sky seems to be a roof to the earth, separating it from higher and serener regions beyond. In old times they thought that it might be frozen air in which stars had been imbedded, and beneath which the sun and moon, made for the purpose of giving light to man, performed their daily rising and setting. This crystalline firmament parted the world of waters above from the earthly world of waters below. It was also the floor of heaven. The poets exhausted their imagination in depicting the splendors of this empyrean abode, the habitation of celestial beings and of the immortal gods.

Not, then, without surprise does man assure himself that he can not trust his eyes; that the sky is only an illusion; and that for distances infinite in his appreciation there is nothing but space and stars.

The atmosphere is then a shell of gas, or rather a mixture of gases, enveloping the earth. It does not extend indefinitely, but its limit is reached at a height of less than fifty miles. Though in one sense invisible, and supposed in the old times to be altogether of a spiritual nature, it is now known to have weight like other material things, and therefore to exert pressure. On every square inch of the surface upon which it rests it bears with a pressure of about fifteen pounds.

Fifty miles it extends upward, becoming thinner and thinner, and at that distance it ends. But to the earth's centre there are nearly four thousand miles. So, if we compare the earth with the atmosphere, they bear about the same proportion to each other that a peach does to the down that covers it. The color of the sky is the blue tint of oxygen gas, one of the chief ingredients of the air.

Besides oxygen there are a great many other aerial substances in the atmosphere, for it must necessarily be the receptacle of every vaporous substance formed on the earth. To such substances the designation of gases has been given, because until recent times they were considered to be of a spiritual character: the word gas is a corruption of geist or ghost. It was generally thought that these principles could take on a bodily form: that they secreted themselves, like genii or apparitions, in pits and caves, suffocating laborers who intruded on their privacy: in mines they guarded treasures. There was abundant evidence that they had often been seen in such solitary places as dwarfs of grotesque appearance, with leathery ears hanging down to their shoulders, and clad in garments of gray cloth.

But we can not altogether rely on human testimony, no matter how copious or respectable it may be. Men now generate gases in glass retorts, collect them in bell jars, fasten them up in bottles, analyze them, combine them with one another. They have no spiritual qualities; they are only matter.

Composed of such ingredients, the air presses on the body of every man with a weight of thirty thousand pounds; yet, wonderful to be said, we do not feel it. Its particles adhere so lightly to each other that motions are very easily established in it, and hence arise breezes and tempests. The swiftness and destructiveness of the latter may impress us with an idea that they are of a supernatural origin; but the poetic angel, who

> "Rides in the whirlwind and directs the storm,"

is, in truth, the warmth of the sun. This warmth, expanding the lower strata of the atmosphere, establishes upward currents, which, influenced by the rotation of the earth on her axis, produce the trade winds that blow eternally in the tropical seas, or, by neutralizing one another, give rise to the tropical calms. On similar physical principles are explained land and sea breezes: they are due to the alternate warming and cooling of the land. The monsoons of the Indian Ocean are traced to the heating of the continents of Africa and Asia alternately. Tornadoes are discs of air whirling round a vertical or somewhat inclined axis, which is carried forward with the storm. In days of old the mariner offered sacrifices to Æolus and Neptune, the gods of the winds and the sea, to preserve his ship from foundering; but now he observes his barometer, and, relying on the published theory of hurricanes, finds safety for himself by sailing out of their way.

Meteorology, less advanced than many other of the sciences, has not yet freed itself completely from the supernatural. The rainy and the dry seasons, the trade winds and calms of the tropics, have been successfully referred to physical causes and clearly explained. In temperate climates there is so much apparent irregularity, that vicissitudes of the weather seem hardly to take place in the necessities of the case and in an inevitable way. But in what parallel of latitude is it that physical agencies end and supernatural ones begin? Men have not yet clearly learned that the course of Nature will never be changed at their entreaty; they do not yet understand that their business is, by exercising the reason that has been given them, to attain foreknowledge of coming events, and arrange their affairs accordingly.

Besides the obvious and sometimes violent movements in the air, there are others of an invisible kind. They are connected with sounds. The ancients feigned that Echo, a nymph who was the daughter of Aer and Tellus, indulging in an unrequited love, pined away until nothing was left but her voice, which still may be heard in rocky solitudes and unfrequented places, once her familiar haunts.

But sounds are only motion. Two things are needful for their perception—vibrating particles to originate, and an elastic medium to convey them. Perhaps it may seem wonderful that the air, which is commonly that medium, though permitting the onward rush of a sound at a rate of 1089 feet in a second, is itself so nearly motionless that not even the motes floating in the sunbeam are disturbed by it, nor the ascending smoke of a chimney that the feeblest breeze could dissipate. That wonder may, however, cease, when we recall what we have seen when a long cord tied at one end is shaken up and down at the other; waves run along it, though the cord keeps its place: or when, in the harvest season, the wind presses on the ripe ears, imparting to them a bowing motion, undulations pass swiftly across the field: it is only a phantom-form that is moving. And so with the air; a wave-like form rushes through it, though it is in reality motionless in its mass.

According as the vibrating body varies its quickness of movement, the note emitted by it changes. The number of times it must beat back and forth to produce a given note has been ascertained by many curious experiments. It may be as low as 32 or as high as 24,000 in a second. Two sounds encountering one another may give rise, as one would anticipate, to an increased effect; but they may also totally neutralize one another, producing absolute silence, and that, no matter how loud they may have been: they are said to interfere. The mechanism of that interference is understood.

To produce the sounds that are necessary for intercommunication among the higher animals, and particularly the speech of man, it might be supposed that some complicated and elaborate contrivance must needs be resorted to. This object is, however, accomplished by merely employing, on its escape from the system, the wasted product of respiration, the breath, which, as it issues outward through the respiratory passages, sets in motion a simple mechanism, and thereby originates all the exquisite modulations of song and all the impressive utterances of speech. Is it not admirable, that thus out of dead and apparently useless matter results of so high an order, materially and mentally, are obtained?

Are not all the inventions of musical notation and alphabetical writing admirable? They enable man to reproduce sounds and their predetermined succession, thereby rekindling sentimental feeling, and conveying knowledge from one generation to another.

From the atmosphere and its phenomena we may turn to the sea. It covers nearly three fourths of the earth's surface, and seems to be a fitting emblem of omnipotence and infinity. Dealing with it as we have dealt with the air, and referring it to the dimensions of the earth, we find that it is nothing more than a mere film resting in shallow cavities on the surface of the earth. The varnish that covers a globe represents its relative size not inadequately.

The color of the sea varies very much at different times and in different localities. It exhibits shades of red, green, and blue, its particular tint depending on the aspect of the sky or clouds—sometimes on the color of its bed, sometimes on the condition of the water itself, as affected by turbidity or by the presence of an infinite number of small aquatic animals, certain species of which often make it phosphorescent by night. Its temperature is different in different latitudes, though a complete correspondence in this respect is not to be anticipated, on account of the facility with which currents are established in it, analogous to winds in the atmosphere. Making due allowance for this, it may be said that its surface temperature varies from about 85° in the torrid zone to the freezing point in the Polar Sea. From the circumstance of its containing so much saline matter, its specific gravity is greater than that of pure water: at the equator it is 1.028. This density necessarily varies with the rate at which superficial evaporation under the influence of the sun is taking place. As the atmosphere is a general receptacle for gases and vapors disengaged from the earth, so the sea is a general receptacle for soluble matter discharged into it by rivers. Among such substances common salt greatly predominates: it constitutes more than three fourths of the entire solid amount.

In the same manner in which it establishes currents in the air by occasioning expansion, solar heat likewise gives rise to currents in the sea. In this instance, however, the action is not of so purely physical a kind as in the other, for a chemical change taking place indirectly modifies the result. This chemical change is an evaporation of pure water, which leaves the sea a more concentrated salt solution than before. Its effect is therefore in some degree to counteract the expansion of the water by warmth; for the sun-rays being able to penetrate several feet below the surface, correspondingly raise the temperature of that portion, which expands and becomes lighter; but, simultaneously, surface evaporation tends to make the water heavier. Notwithstanding this, in a general way currents are established, answering to winds in the air. Of these the Gulf Stream is the most interesting example.

The mechanical action of the sun-rays in occasioning currents is thus effected through the expansion of the water, of which the warm portions ascend to the surface, colder portions from beneath setting in to supply their place. These currents, both hot and cold, are of course affected by the diurnal rotation of the earth, the action being, in principle, the same as that occurring in the winds. They exert so great an influence as conveyers of heat, as to disturb the ordinary climate relations depending on the sun's position.

But not only as a liquid does water exist; it can assume other forms, becoming solid in ice and aerial in steam. In what does the difference of these states consist? Ordinary experience must at all times have indicated that these changes depend on temperature;

but it was not until the last century that the true relation was distinctly made out. The intrinsic difference between water and ice is this, that water contains about 140 degrees of heat more than ice, and that this heat is imperceptible to the thermometer. When, therefore, ice turns into water, the 140 degrees of heat must be imparted, and when water turns into ice they must be taken away. Moreover, the intrinsic difference between water and its vapor, or steam, is this; that though they may be at the same temperature, steam contains about 1000 degrees of heat more than water, which large amount—enough, indeed, to make a solid body red hot—is altogether imperceptible by the thermometer. When water turns into steam these thousand degrees of heat must be furnished, and when steam is condensed into water they must be taken away. This discovery was not only of importance scientifically, it was also connected with the great invention of the last century—the steam-engine, which has revolutionized the industry of the world.

What has not that invention done for America? At this moment it more than doubles our laboring population, it makes available our vast river system, and in the railway binds the most distant parts of the Nation together. What would this continent have been if we had possessed no cheaper and better sources of power than that of animals, or of falling water, or of the wind? The application of an apparently abstruse fact connected with latent heat, and the relations of vapors and liquids to one another, has been essentially necessary to the development of our Western civilization.

The invention of the steam-engine was followed by the discovery of the compound nature of water. From the most primitive times that liquid had been considered to be a simple undecomposable body. It was one of the four elements of antiquity. But soon after the discovery of two very important gases, Oxygen and Hydrogen, a suspicion that it is composed of them began to be entertained. The invention of the Voltaic battery finally and decisively settled that point, the compound nature of water being placed beyond contradiction. There can be no exaggeration of the importance of this discovery. It may be affirmed to have been the starting-point of the wonderful development of modern chemistry.

The sun's heat causes evaporation to take place from the entire surface of the sea, but to a different degree in different latitudes. In the torrid zone, where the heat is greatest, the quantity thus raised is a maximum, and from that region the amount declines north and south toward the poles. It is to be understood that the water thus vaporized is pure, and contains no saline matter. In consequence of this different degree of vaporization, it necessarily follows that the percentage of salt is greatest at the equator, and there the specific gravity would be very much higher were it not for the more elevated temperature. As to the nature of evaporation, the earlier chemists imagined that it was altogether due to atmospheric agency, the air dissolving more moisture as its temperature is higher.

In the Patristic philosophy it was supposed that the quantity of water in the sea was once far greater than at present, sufficient, indeed, to overflow the mountains, but that it had been removed and the land dried by the agency of a wind. The quantity of material substance on the globe has never diminished; it is the same now as it was in the beginning. Such a diminution could not take place without causing an alteration in the length of the year. Evaporation is due not to the agency of the air, but to heat, heat alone determining the quantity of vapor that can exist in a given space, that quantity being the same whether the space is a void or already occupied by other gases. If the temperature rises, the amount of vapor that can exist in such a space increases; if the temperature declines, it diminishes. All this is dependent on the fact that the elastic force of a vapor increases with its temperature, and that for every temperature there is a density for the vapor which can not be exceeded without liquefaction ensuing. This point is known as that of maximum density. It was by a thorough comprehension of the principles herein involved that Watt was led to invent the low-pressure steam-engine, in which he accomplished the apparently paradoxical result of condensing the steam without cooling the cylinder.

Thus there is raised from the sea and from the damp surface of the land a quantity of fresh water, every day, answering to the supply of solar heat. It rises in the warm current, ascending in a perfectly invisible state, retaining that condition until it comes to regions the temperature of which is low enough to surpass the point of maximum density and occasion condensation. As this takes place in the upper strata, the liquid water, as it forms, is in globules of perhaps $\frac{1}{50,000}$ of an inch in size. Their misty aggregate is a cloud.

Clouds, while thus floating in the air, if their dimensions are not too great, so as to overshadow the canopy, become beautiful objects as reflectors of the sun's light, and thus borrowing tints and brilliancy from his rays. They may either dissolve away by coming into warmer or dryer spaces, or their minute spherules, coalescing together, may descend to the ground as rain. Water descending as rain is perhaps the purest offered to us by nature, yet it is far from being chemically pure. The rain-drops dissolve out of the air portions of its various gaseous ingredients, and become especially contaminated by dust and organic matter disseminated through it. Pure water can only be obtained by careful distillation in vessels made of platinum, silver, or gold.

Rain, falling on the earth, sinks through the pores and crevices to issue forth again in certain localities as springs. Before the water thus emerges it has become still farther contaminated by dissolving whatever soluble materials chance to be in its way. Each spring discharging its waters through a little branch, these successively coalesce with one another, forming streams larger and larger until they become a river. In that manner a section of country is drained through its lowlands and valleys, the river making its way down its incline, and eventually delivering its waters into the sea. Thus, by the heat of the sun and gravitation conjointly, the water passes through a complete cycle. From the sea it arose, to the sea it inevitably returns.

But, though water thus derived from the sea returns thereto ultimately with inevitable certainty, a portion is intercepted and delayed in its course, to discharge very important offices in the mechanical and organic phenomena of the earth.

As respects its mechanical functions, space would fail me if I were to consider them in detail, or to attempt to show how greatly, in its liquid state, water is the agent that modifies the surface of the globe. There falls not a drop of rain which does not disintegrate and disturb portions of the soil; there flows not a stream which does not carry solid matter into the sea. It is for geology to contemplate the amazing aggregate of detritus thus removed from continents, diminishing their height and filling up the bed of the sea; to consider the effects in colder climates arising from the freezing of water and the properties of ice in the act of solidification—the expansion tending to pulverize the soil effectually, as agriculturists well know. In such masses as glaciers and icebergs the mechanical effects are of no little scientific interest. The vaporous condition and changes from it are subjects which engross a large portion of meteorology; for such events as the condensation of atmospheric moisture into rain, snow, hail, can not occur without enormous disturbances in the pressure and other relations of the air, giving rise to many imposing meteorological events.

But of all meteorological phenomena, undoubtedly the most surprising are the displays of atmospheric electricity. What can be more beautiful than the fantastic, the ever-changing movements of the Aurora? what more imposing than the flash of lightning? Not without reason have men in all ages looked upon the former as glimpses of the movements of angels, and upon the latter as being the weapon of God.

Scientific discovery has not only removed these prodigies from the domain of the supernatural, it has also made the agent concerned in their production available for the purposes of man. When Franklin, with a boy's kite, drew down the lightning from heaven, there was a great moral as well as physical result. Human opinions were modified, the power of man was increased.

It is an illustration of the excellence and fertility of modern methods of investigation, that the phenomena of attraction displayed by amber, which had been known and neglected for two thousand years, subsequently, in one tenth of that time, led to surprising consequences. First, it was shown that there are many other bodies which will act in like manner; then came the invention of the electrical machine; the discovery of electrical repulsion and the spark; the differences of conductibility in bodies; the two apparent species of electricity, vitreous and resinous; the general law of attraction and repulsion; the wonderful phenomena of the Leyden vial and the electric shock; the demonstration of the identity of lightning and electricity; the means of protecting buildings and ships by rods; the velocity of electric movement, immense distances being passed through in an inappreciable time; the theory of one fluid and that of two; the mathematical discussion of all the phenomena, first on one and then on the other of those doctrines; the invention of the torsion balance; the determination that the attractive and repulsive forces followed the law of the inverse squares; the conditions of distribution on conductors; the elucidation of the phenomena of induction. At length, when discovery seemed to be pausing, the facts of galvanism were announced in Italy. Up to this time it was thought that the most certain sign of the death of an animal was its inability to exhibit muscular contraction; but now it was shown that muscular movements could be excited in those that were dead and even mutilated. Then quickly followed the invention of the Voltaic pile. Who could have believed that the twitching of a frog's leg, in the experiments of Galvani, would give rise, in a very few years, to the establishment beyond all question of the compound nature of water, separating its constituents from one another—would lead to the deflagration and dissipation, in a vapor, of metals that can hardly be melted in a furnace—would show that the solid earth we tread upon is an oxide—yield new metals light enough to swim upon water, and even seem to set it on fire—produce the most brilliant of all artificial lights, rivaling, if not excelling, in its intolerable splendor the noontide sun—would occasion a complete revolution in chemistry, compelling that science to accept new ideas and even a new nomenclature—that it would give us the power of making magnets capable of lifting more than a ton, cast a light on that riddle of ages, the pointing of the mariner's compass north and south, and explain the mutual attraction or repulsion of magnetic needles—that it would enable us to form exquisitely in metal casts of all kinds of objects of art, and give workmen a means of performing gilding and silvering without risk to their health—that it would suggest to the evil disposed the forging of bank-notes, the sophisticating of jewelry, and be invaluable in the uttering of false coinage—that it would carry the messages of commerce and friendship instantaneously across continents or under oceans, and "waft a sigh from Indus to the Pole!"

Yet that is only a part of what Galvani's experiment, carried out by modern methods, has actually done. Could there be a more brilliant instance of their power, a brighter earnest of the future of physical philosophy?

The Venetians brought the use of the magnetic needle, for the purposes of navigation, from China. The properties of the loadstone had been known both in Europe and Asia from very remote times. It attracts pieces of iron, imparts its own qualities permanently to tempered steel, and, if floated on water or poised on a pivot, points north and south.

This pointing, however, in most places is not accurate; there is a certain deviation or declination. When Columbus made his first voyage across the Atlantic, he found that there was a position about a hundred miles west of the Azores where the pointing was true. To the meridian passing through this place the designation of the line of no variation was given. The Papal government, considering this to be a natural boundary between the east and west hemispheres of the earth, made it the dividing-line between the Spanish and Portuguese possessions.

But, though it was subsequently ascertained that this adjudication was founded on a misconception, and that the line of no variation is unceasingly moving, a surprising consequence followed—the circumnavigation of the earth.

Science is full of wonders. The movements of a poised steel needle overthrew opinions that had been endorsed by the highest human authorities. It was no longer possible to maintain that the earth is a flat surface covered over with the dome of the sky; it was no longer possible to deny that it is a globe revolving round a central sun.

A piece of rubbed amber attracts a straw: that little fact, thoroughly investigated, leads to the invention of the electric telegraph, and men communicate with one another instantaneously across continents and under the bottom of oceans. The sunshine coming through an angular fragment of glass produces a play of colors, and the rainbow, in the old times thought to be God's weapon resting against the clouds, is explained. A straight stick dipped into water seems as if it were broken, and it follows that we see the sun before he has risen and after he has set—that, with the exception of the one that happens to be overhead, all the stars in the sky are imagined to be in places where in reality they are not. A ball of glass, if looked through, magnifies objects, a concave fragment diminishes them: that leads to the invention of spectacles, and the giving of sight to the blind. Some scratches on a polished piece of metal set in the sun-rays exhibit gaudy colors like a peacock's feather, and it follows that light added to light may produce total darkness. A bar of iron, cooled, becomes too small to occupy completely a space it had previously filled, and therefore the apparent constancy in the size of familiar objects turns out to be a delusion: they are larger by day than they are by night, they are smaller in winter than in summer; and if a cloud passes over the sun all things in the shade diminish, but they regain their size as soon as his beams are restored. How wonderful is the Stereoscope, through which, if we look at two flat pictures, we see but one, yet that stands out with an air of solidity and with the deception of perspective! How wonderful the Microscope, which enables us to discern, in living specks that could creep through the eye of a needle, elaborate and complicated organs for respiration, for circulation, for digestion, as perfect as those of the elephant! How wonderful the Telescope, which has revealed to us countless myriads of worlds in the abysses of space, and has forever destroyed the doctrine that the universe was made for man! How wonderful the Spectroscope, which teaches us the material composition of those distant orbs, what metals, what gases they contain, and demonstrates to us the manner in which systems of worlds arise!

But it is in vain to go on. I remarked, a few pages back, that the facts of science exceed the capacity of any one book. It is in vain to attempt to do justice to the vast accumulation, in vain to try to set forth the importance of that glorious monument to the intellect of man.

Why is it that in Europe the doctrines connected with these facts, instead of being welcomed with delight, have had to fight their way? Why is it that those who have revealed them suffer obloquy, in some instances have suffered death?

Why should men be angry when they are told that the sky is not an empyrean floor, but only an optical deception, there being nothing but space and stars beyond us; that the earth is not a flat and immovable plate, but a swiftly rushing globe; that the rising and setting of the sun and the moon are all a delusion; that there are people on the other side of the earth whose feet are planted toward ours; that the world was not made yesterday, but is myriads of centuries old; that the occurrence of death is not a recent event, unnumbered individuals—nay, even unnumbered races of animated forms having passed away before the first man lived; that climate modifies plants and animals, and even men; that the planet we inhabit, if seen from the sun, round which it revolves, would seem like a little spark; that if considered with other orbs, its companions in the universe, it is as insignificant as a mote that dances in the sunbeam along with its companion motes; that the motions of the bodies of the solar system take place under a mathematical necessity, and that the world is governed by law?

What is there, I ask, in such things as these to provoke the resentment of man? Why is it that he has visited with punishment those who first suggested many of them, and looks with jealous suspicion on those who receive them as true? Why is it that in presence of the telegraph, the steamship, the locomotive, the printing-press, photography, and all the unspeakable triumphs of science in his behalf—triumphs the immediate results of the investigation and conclusions of science—why is it that he tries to stamp an odium on those who devote themselves to the true interpretation of Nature?

Is it any answer to say that, some fifteen hundred years ago, there was a Roman general who seized imperial power from his competitors, and whose political necessities were such that he had to inaugurate this untoward course? Because he did it, therefore we must do it! That is the only answer that can be made.

How different would it have been with the Papacy, had it in its day of power, instead of resisting the advancement of human knowledge, fostered and favored it! How different if, instead of perpetually looking backward, it had looked forward, and put itself forth as the promoter of intellectual development!

It falls to the lot of the American Republic to perform the duty that was declined by Rome. Freedom for man, so far as his personal acts are concerned, is already secured; but how much still remains to be done for freedom of thought!

A country that owes its almost miraculous material prosperity to its frank acceptance of the idea that man can comprehend Nature and subjugate her to his use—a country that furnishes the most brilliant instance of the conquest of Nature by man, owes it to itself and owes it to the world to stand forth the Defender and Protector of thought.

Western Europe, to which in this particular we owe so much, labors under the dead weight of vast ecclesiastical establishments: their influences ramify through all the ranks of society. The tendency given to them by the Byzantine sovereigns and by the Roman Papacy is unchangeable. They will ever continue to be what they have always been—the determined antagonists of science.

In those countries every onward step that science makes implies a conflict. In America, where there is no such dead weight, and where the genius of the public institutions is so different, the progress of thought ought to be free.

But is it so? Is there no insidious molestation? In a land that is netted with telegraph wires, and possessing, in a cheap post-office system, unparalleled means for the dissemination of thought, is it well that a new fact or a new doctrine should be received with a jealous eye, that looks more to an accordance with existing interests than to absolute truth?

Intellectual freedom must be secured as completely as the rights of property and personal liberty have been already secured. Philosophical opinions and scientific discoveries are entitled to be judged of by their truth, not by their relation to existing interests. The motion of the earth round the sun, the antiquity of the globe, the origin of species, are doctrines which have had to force their way, not against philosophical opposition, but opposition of a totally different nature. And yet the interests which resisted them so strenuously have received no damage from their establishment beyond that consequent on the discredit of having so resisted them.

There is no literary crime greater than that of exciting a social and especially a theological odium against ideas that are purely scientific, none against which the disapproval of every educated man ought to be more strongly expressed. The republic of letters owes it to its own dignity to tolerate no longer offenses of that kind.

## CHAPTER IV.

### ON THE NATURAL COURSE OF NATIONAL DEVELOPMENT.

*The Organization, Development, and Government of the Natural World are shown to involve a continual tendency to concentration of power, and the conferring of a dominant control on Intelligence.*

*This principle applies in the case of human societies during their political development. A comparison is instituted between the European method of government through the Morals, and the American of government through the Intellect. It is illustrated by the history of England, taken as a type of the former, and by the history of the United States, taken as a type of the latter.*

*It follows, from the Intellectual method adopted, that America must be the scene of a future conflict of Ideas. Their action, reaction, and modifications are alluded to, and the scientific tendency to unity of opinion pointed out.*

*And, finally, the analogies between the Italian ecclesiastical system and the American civil system are referred to.*

*The general object of the chapter is to show that in all durable human associations there is a natural, an inevitable tendency to the concentration of power; and that, so far from this being in antagonism to democratical institutions, it is their legitimate and unavoidable result.*

The Book of Nature, the Visible World, is always open to us for our instruction and guidance. From its pages we may gather lessons respecting the social progress of man. With silent emphasis it appeals to our understanding, whatever may be the political opinions we entertain, whatever the religious faith we prefer.

It is no metaphor, but a reality, that the life of human societies is typified by the life of plants and animals. Throughout the whole world of organization the scheme of Nature is the same.

I intend in this chapter, as clearly as I can, to present that scheme of progress; to explain its intention, its aim—to show how human societies must comport themselves and follow the footprints of Nature.

As we have seen, the progress of such societies is directed in part by physical influences, and in part by the force of Ideas, but it is always determined by law. American history furnishes signal examples of these truths. It shows us that climate has produced constitutional differences between the man of the North and the man of the South; that it has made them think differently and act differently; that it has brought into antagonism the enthusiastic impulsiveness of the one and the inexorable perseverance of the other.

Does not that history also illustrate the political force of an Idea?

And what is that Idea? That there shall exist on this continent one Republic, great and indivisible, whose grandeur shall eclipse the grandeur of Rome in its brightest days—sovereign among the Powers of the earth; so ruling in truth, in wisdom, in justice, in force, that every human being, no matter how obscure or desolate he may be, may find in it a refuge and protector; that every government, from the Atlantic Ocean eastward to the Chinese Seas, no matter how strong it may be, shall listen with attention to its suggestions.

To convert that vision of future greatness into a reality, organic laws that are at the basis of personal liberty have been, without a murmur or question, for a season surrendered; a navy has been created, no inadequate antagonist to the navies of the world; an army has been organized equal to that of any of the greatest military monarchies of Europe. For four years in succession eight hundred millions of dollars have been spent. Rome never would have permitted a divided empire in Italy: the Lion will tolerate no competitor in his desert, the Eagle will endure no rival in the air.

The first act in the drama of American national life is over. There are many good men who look lingeringly on the past, expecting its wished-for return. The past never returns. With our high aspirations, our enormous military and industrial power, it is for us to turn our faces to the future. There is indeed a manifest destiny before us.

There is a course through which we *must* go. Let us cast from ourselves the untrue, the unworthy belief that the will of man determines the events of this world. National life is shaped by something far higher than that; it is shaped by a stern logic of events.

In the Dark Ages they are said to have had magical mirrors, on which, if a man looked, he might see reflected all the future events of his life. Nature holds up her enchanted mirror to us: in the moving images and changing scenery it presents we may discern what we are about to be.

When Alexander the Great, the ablest man of European antiquity, was engaged in the conquest of Asia, he gave to Aristotle, who had been his instructor, a million of dollars and the services of several thousand men, to enable him to write "A History of Animals." The organic world was ransacked, dissections were made, habits were observed, descriptions written, drawings executed. The view of Aristotle, that all animals constitute a vast but a continuous chain—characterized by Humboldt, in our own times, as "very grand"—fell, however, out of sight after the death of Greece and the dissolution of the Roman Empire, the hybrid population subsequently inhabiting the shores of the Mediterranean being wholly unable to rise to such magnificent conceptions. They were occupied with baser thoughts.

Not until our own century have men been able to recover and appreciate that great idea. At length it has been thoroughly incorporated into modern physiology. We shall see, to our surprise, that it is one of the keys of history.

To the eye of the Physiologist all animated forms present themselves as one continuous chain—the Organic Series he calls them. Commencing in lowly beginnings, that are doubtfully separated from the vegetable world, they rise by continuous, by unbroken stages to the highest—that is, to man. It is the object of his study to ascertain the construction, the anatomy of each of the essential links in that organic chain, and to observe the result, for the habits and instincts of these various beings are the consequences of their conformation. This work of prodigious labor accomplished, it is his hope to be able to attain to a comprehension of the whole scheme—to appreciate the creative thought that pervades it—that has, in fact, called it into existence; a study surpassing in its sublimity even the grandeur of astronomy, and, like it, teaching us to appreciate the thoughts and intentions of the Sovereign Constructor of the universe.

Though very far from its completion, this study already enables us to discern, it may be darkly, the grand plan. In this, the twilight of the breaking morning of human intelligence, we begin to perceive some of the bolder features of that landscape which hereafter, in the noontide of human reason, will be spread out, a vast panorama, before our descendants.

Already we trace the course of Nature, we see the intention of this world of life.

At the commencement of the vista of organization the forms are obscure, in structure simple, in habit low. Like the contrivances invented by man, they are mere automatons. As in a machine, if we touch a given spring a given motion will be produced, so these, acting unconsciously, move under the impulse inflicted. But, by a gradual unfolding of structure, part developing from part and function emerging from function, a higher stage is reached—to automatism instinct is added. The innumerable tribes exemplifying this state excite our admiration by the orderly manner in which they accomplish their predestined works, the bee building its comb, the spider constructing his web. But among these it is to be particularly observed that the qualities of the more lowly tribes are still present; automatism has not been displaced by instinct, but instinct has been, as it were, superposed, and both co-exist. Still looking along the chain as we advance, once more we recognize a repetition of the same process, or, more correctly, the gradual addition of something higher. Instinct is unfolding itself into Intelligence. The animated being shows reasoning powers, at every successive rising link increasing in precision and perfection—the adaptation of purposed means to the accomplishment of wished-for ends. The Dog forms his plans; his master relates with admiration how he has watched him proceed in carrying them out, persuading himself that there is something approaching to wisdom even in the brute. Here again, as in the former case, the new faculty has not destroyed the old one, but intelligence is co-existing both with instinct and with automatism.

This, then, is the sum of the matter. From a purely mechanical state, appropriately termed automatism, a higher state, the Instinctive, is educed; from that, in its turn, a still higher—the Intelligent. And, viewing the organic series from end to end, this is the affirmation that may be made: the course of Nature is for the development and concentration of Intellect.

I have abstained from burdening this description with anatomical discoveries and details; they are scarcely suitable for the present occasion. In that respect it is perhaps enough to say that the structure connected with these wonderful acts is the nervous system. In the lowliest tribes it is, as it were, rudimentary, its action purely mechanical. Next, offshoots of that rudiment appear, dedicated to special purposes—ganglia, as anatomists call them—intended to receive the impressions of sound and of light. Step by step the development, the concentration proceeds, until a most important stage is eventually reached. In the region of the head a special mass, or rather pair of masses, appears, having direct connections of its own, by means of nerves, with all parts of the body.

This organ, the cephalic ganglia, soon indicates what it is for—a control and government over all the rest. The impressions they receive are carried to it; its volitions are sent back to them.

Here we may pause a moment to make this significant remark—every thing is tending to a concentration of power.

In man each of these typical parts is present, and discharges the duties we have described. There is the spinal cord, acting automatically; there are the same special ganglia for breathing and swallowing; there are the same parts for hearing, sight, smell; the same governing ganglia. He therefore combines the automatic and the instinctive apparatus.

But it is to be especially observed that, as we advance toward him through animals which, though inferior to him, are high in the scale of life, another most important part appears: we recognize it as the brain. The moment we discern that, reasoning powers are present, the degree of intelligence becoming more strikingly marked as the development of the new organ is greater.

In the nervous system of man there are, therefore, three essentially distinct parts—the spinal cord, the ganglia of sense, the brain. Of the first, the action is purely automatic; by its aid we walk without bestowing a thought on our movements from place to place; we breathe without knowing it. The second is the place of reception of the impressions of external things—light, sound, odors; it is also the seat of consciousness; it is the instinctive mechanism. The third, the brain, is anatomically distinct. It is the theatre of ideas, the realm of thought, the instrument through which the mind works.

There is, therefore, a regular progression, a definite improvement in this ascending gradation of animal life from the lowest to the superior; the plan never varying, but being persistently carried out. It begins with automatism, it advances to instinct, it reaches intelligence. In fishes a true brain first appears; it has received an improvement in reptiles; it advances still farther in birds. In that same order the rate of intelligence advances. Man presents the utmost perfection thus far attained. His brain has reached a maximum organization by a continued and unbroken process of development.

If I have made myself understood in this orderly development of the ascending scale of animals, I shall not be misunderstood in obscurely referring to what, if the occasion permitted, I might dwell upon in detail. Identically the same orderly progress is recognized in the life of individual man. The primitive trace, as it faintly appears in the germinal membrane, marks out the automatic apparatus; that is followed by the instinctive, for not until the twelfth week of life have we reached the condition permanently presented by birds; a little later the brain is brought into a complete state; and thus it appears that man proceeds through the same predetermined succession of forms.

But that is not all. The biography of the earth, the life of the entire globe, corresponds to this progress of the Individual, to this orderly advance of the animal series, as it is the glory of Geology to have shown. Commencing with the oldest rocks that furnish organic remains, and advancing to the most recent, we recognize the same continuous course of construction.

What is the object, the end of all these successive phases of life? Intellectual development.

Ask the Anatomist; he points you to the career of individual man, from the first dawn of life to its close, and tells you that every thing is aiming at Intellect.

Ask the Physiologist; he bids you consider the vast series of animated forms inhabiting the earth with us. He affirms that we are reflected in them; and that, as their advancement in the predetermined direction is greater, so is the order of their intelligence higher.

Ask the Geologist, and he will declare that those conclusions hold good in the history of the earth, and that there has been an orderly improvement in intellectual power among the beings who have successively inhabited it.

The sciences, therefore, affirm that the great aim of Nature is to reach controlling intellect. They proclaim that the successive stages of every individual, from its earliest rudiment to maturity; the numberless organic beings now living with us and constituting the animal series; the orderly appearance of that grand succession which, in the slow lapse of time, has emerged—all these three great lines of the manifestation of life furnish not only evidence, but also proof of the dominion of invariable law. The principle is to advance from automatism to instinct, from instinct to intelligence. In man himself the three distinct modes of life occur in an epochal order, through childhood to the most perfect state; and this holding good for the individual, since it is physiologically impossible to separate him from the race, what holds good for the one must hold good for the other too. Hence man is truly the archetype of society. His development is the model of what social progress must be.

What, then, is the conclusion inculcated by these doctrines as regards the social progress of great communities? It is, that all political institutions, imperceptibly or visibly, spontaneously or purposely, should tend to the improvement and organization of National Intellect.

A nation may from this grand example trace out its proper course. The body politic, like the body personal, must be ruled by its intellect. It is of no use to affirm that the foot, or the hand, or the stomach can guide as well as the head. The social machine is composed of parts, each of which has its own appropriate duty to do.

Already enlightened governments discern the truth of this. They rest their expectations, their hopes of society, on universal education, compulsory if need be, to give to each one the opportunity of improvement up to the point that Nature has permitted for him.

But education is a term of wide import. That demanded by modern times must represent the contemporaneous knowledge of the race. The defect of our present systems is this—that they look too much to the past; they deal too much with the doubtful, too little with the exact.

A dozen rich gentlemen may meet together and proceed to build a railroad across the continent, or lay a telegraphic wire under the Atlantic Ocean. They may do whatever is possible to the omnipotence of wealth. But, though all Americans should constitute themselves a joint-stock company, they never, by any votes or any resolves, could call into existence a great soldier, a great lawgiver, a great philosopher. They could never create a Newton, a Milton, an Alexander. Talent is a God-given gift.

Then, though public education is an eminent advantage, it is far from being every thing. The advancement of a nation to greatness demands that not only shall every individual be instructed, but that the career shall be open to talent. That principle was thoroughly understood by the great Italian statesmen who for so many centuries controlled European affairs. They found out and fostered intellect wherever they could. How often did they take the cowl from the monk, and give him in exchange a mitre! It signified nothing to them that the greatest churchman might have come from the lowest dregs of society. Wealth, and splendors, and worldly dignity they could amply bestow; Intellect they were obliged to find.

For stability to be attained, a nation must submit to be controlled by its reason; it must organize its intellect, it must concentrate it.

There are but three powers that can organize the world—theology, literature, science. Europe has tried the first; her present condition shows what is the utmost it can do. China has tried the second, and has become conceited and exclusive. It has been truly affirmed that for these purposes science has this advantage over literature, that it admits of universal communion.

Let us not, however, fall into the delusion of expecting what will never happen from such social organization; the very term itself implies, on the one hand, superiority; on the other, subordination. Do what we may, no organization, no education will ever make all men alike. By far the most numerous portion of our race must devote itself to labor, scarcely ever learning any thing except what concerns its daily toil: whatever improvement it attains to is by mere imitation. It follows its hereditary instincts, having no idea of progress, none of development. Governed by external influences and by its own appetites, it can neither combine nor generalize. Its movements altogether depend on the unrecognized influence of external agents. That vast mass, like a cloud, drifts along to its destiny in an invisible wind.

In our nation there has been a period of material prosperity, of which I think we shall all agree in saying that it has had no parallel in the world. Wealth, honorably acquired, has poured in upon us until we have become blinded to all things else. Here and there a thoughtful man may be found who has seen with misgivings that it is not spiritual, but physical aspirations that have heretofore predominated among us. How true it is that, for a nation to be great, it must aim at something above its animal nature!

We are in the act of transition from the animal to the intellectual. War, civil war, with its dread punishments, is not without its uses. In no other school than that of war can society learn subordination, in no other can it be made to appreciate order. It may be true, as has been affirmed, that men secretly love to obey those whom they feel to be their superiors intellectually. In military life they learn to practice that obedience openly.

I turn from the hideous contemplation of a disorganization of the Republic, each state, and county, and town setting up for itself, and the continent swarming with the maggots bred from the dead body politic. I turn from that to a future I see in prospect—an imperial race organizing its intellect, concentrating it, and voluntarily submitting to be controlled by its reason; a race despising that low grade of life into which its enemies have tauntingly said that it has descended, and that, like certain base animals, it may be spontaneously dissevered into a multitude of parts, each being as good as any of the rest, and capable of the same obscene separations again.

In thus asserting that in all human communities, as their life advances, there must be a continual tendency to a concentration of power and a development of intellect, I am presenting the conclusions of observers of Nature.

Physiologists say that *growth* is an increase in the size of a structure of any kind, no variation occurring in the character of the fabric or in the functions it discharges; but *differentiation* is an increase involving modification of fabric and assumption of new functions.

The lowest plants simply grow; they increase by

the addition of units or parts of the same kind and having the same office. They have no mutual dependence except that consequent on their mere mechanical union. They may be cut to pieces, and, as we have just observed, each portion is as perfect, as good as the rest. Each individually, and all conjointly, are very low.

But in the highest plants there is something more. At one point roots are put forth, at another leaves, at another flowers. The duty of the root is to hold the plant in the ground, and furnish it with water and some salts; that of the leaves, to procure nutriment from the air; that of the flowers, to reproduce plants of the same kind. These various, these *different* organs have been evolved or differentiated for those purposes.

The same remark applies to animals. In the lowest, breathing, digestion, and all the various other functions needful for life are confusedly blended together, and obscurely discharged by the self-same part. In the highest, special organs, the lungs, the stomach, etc., have been differentiated from the growing mass for these special functions.

Now we must particularly remark the manner in which all this is done. If, for a new purpose, a new organ is wanted, Nature never fashions it in secret or apart, finishing her work by attaching the new product to the structure intended to be improved. Men, when they design to improve a house, bring the necessary materials from elsewhere, and make their addition by attaching it. Not so with Nature. She evolves from what is already pre-existing — there comes an outshoot, not an addition. Thus, in the illustration we have referred to, she makes flowers from parts that, had the differentiation been otherwise, might have been leaves.

It is, as I have said, no metaphor, but a reality, that human societies are typified by plants and animals. Both, in their lowest grades, are aggregates increasing by the addition of parts, each of which is similar, and acts similarly to all its fellows. In a tribe of savages each man does every thing for himself. By degrees special pursuits pass into the hands of particular individuals. The process goes on until three distinct social divisions are established—a laboring class, a trading or transferring class, an intellectual class. Political differentiation has taken place.

Society thus passes through a definite, an orderly succession of changes. It grows at first by the addition of units; then, under internal and external influences, it begins to differentiate.

In individual man how strikingly, also, is the same thing perceived! It is not a mere growth or development alone that occurs; but when that process has gone on to a certain extent, a new condition of things abruptly takes place, a difference in structure, a difference in function suddenly arising—suddenly, yet, as we find when we examine the matter critically, in a necessary and inevitable way; for the new things have issued forth from the old by an insensible shading, so that we can not tell at what time the one ended or when the other began. In spite of the rapidity with which the change may have taken place, we still discern consecutive points bearing a determinate relation to one another. Development thus gives rise to differentiation: they do not stand in an attitude of antagonism.

It is immaterial whether we consider the entire human body in the aggregate, or limit ourselves to the investigation of its constituent parts; whether we describe man existing as a water-breathing, and then abruptly at his first respiration as an air-breathing animal; or whether, descending to minor details, we investigate the structure of his digestive, circulating, absorbing, or other parts, and the duties they discharge. As his development goes on, differentiation in a necessary manner, at determinate epochs, takes place; and thus he proceeds through a multitude of forms in an orderly succession, each form issuing from the preceding one in an unavoidable way. Nor is there any possibility that a single step in the whole progress can be omitted. What better proof can we have of the determinate character of this advance than the fact that it is repeated, with all its peculiarities of epochs and phases, by every individual? The complete and affiliated series of embryonic forms presented in the early period of the life of man is only an exemplification that he is held fast in the grasp of those laws which control all other animals.

So, in communities, development takes place from point to point; it issues in their numerical increase, their geographical spread, their growth. For a while, from year to year, it may offer no point of perceptible change, but at last differentiation occurs—not so abruptly as in the instance of the individual, for the general scale of time has been enlarged. It makes itself manifest by a cessation of the old and an exhibition of the new—by an abandonment of former habits of action, by an appearance of new modes of thought. The society that has passed through such an epoch looks back on its history with surprise, half wondering whether it can be really true that it once concerned itself in actions now appearing so unsuitable and unworthy—that it once was sincerely engaged with mental conceptions now seeming to be so clearly fallacious.

The law of development, known among physiologists as that of Von Bär, and of the truth of which there is now abundant proof, is to the effect that "the heterogeneous arises from the homogeneous by a gradual process of change." Thus, from the starting-point of all living forms—a simple cell—there are unfolded in a proper order successive parts devoted to special duties, and from these, in their turn, in like manner secondary and tertiary subdivisions arise, the duty discharged in the first instance by the aggregate being now accomplished by the special portions, and therefore in a more complete and perfect way.

What thus takes place in the individual also takes place in the nation. We deceive ourselves when we suppose that the process of human affairs is ever disturbed by the intrusion of things that are intrinsically new. Every event, no matter how abruptly it may occur, is, if we carefully consider it, indissolubly affiliated with events that have gone before, and draws in its train others that of necessity follow. In this, as in the former instance, we never encounter the appearance of incongruous things, but all proceeds in an orderly way. Our daily experience assures us that for the success of any human undertaking opportunity is essential. Without that the greatest genius and the greatest exertions are spent in vain. The physiological law of Von Bär holds as good in race advancement as it does in individual. Its action is expressed in both instances in a similar manner.

It is through the general operation of this law that communities emerge from the lowest grades of social life—from that barbarous condition in which all individuals are occupied in all pursuits, and especially excelling in none; in which the avocations of the farm-er, the huntsman, the mechanic, are all equally discharged by each individual. It is through the operation of this law that, as society is advancing in its course from that confused condition in which all things were blended together, that special duties and special avocations begin to emerge; through it the process of partition and separation, as expressed in the different trades and occupations, is continued; through it the skilled labor of civilized communities results. In thus applying a physiological law holding good for the individual to this our social state, we indulge in no fictitious hypothesis. Society is only an aggregate of individuals; whatever affects, whatever regulates each of them, must affect and regulate it also. Its actions are the sum of their actions.

By the light thrown from the history of the individual on that of society, we ascertain the true interpretation of the successive stages in the course of the latter, and determine the value of each of its constituent parts; that, equally in the one as in the other, the first moments are devoted to the necessities of animal existence, and only by degrees does the intellectual begin to emerge. The first phases of life, no matter what may be the scale on which we consider it, individual or social, are essentially vegetative, the operation being, as the advance goes on, to disentangle the intellectual from the clogs that are attached to it, and at last to accomplish its isolation. As by such partitions and separations it increases in purity, it also increases in power, until, in the end, it becomes the authoritative, the governing, and regulating principle, subjecting all other things to its dominion.

We may therefore transfer from the individual to society all those phenomena of equilibrium and movement observed by Physiologists. In the same manner that we see in the individual organic particles in all stages of activity and decline, some subserving one, some another duty, so in society we distinguish between the uses and conditions of different persons. It is to be remembered that Persons are the equivalent of Particles. Notwithstanding this diversity of their functions, all, without any exception, are under the necessity of submitting to the same laws, and therefore run through similar cycles of motion, having a period at which they make their appearance as organic elements, a period at which they enter upon their destined duty, a period of maximum development and force, one also of decline. And as in the individual we find particles of different constitutions arranged in different places for the proper performance of their functions, so the social grades and several occupations of men answer thereto. Seen in this light, it is plain that all have a duty to discharge—a duty not alone to themselves, but to the aggregate of which they form a part, and to the well-being of which they are essential. All, therefore, in one sense, are equal, for each has an indispensable duty allotted, each being equally useful, equally worthy. The intellectual relations of society can not be maintained save by the aid of its organic relations, any more than the intellectual functions of the individual can be successfully accomplished except by the co-operation of the functions of organic life. How is it possible that the brain, in one sense the most noble portion of the human economy, should discharge its duty aright, or even discharge it at all, unless the subordinate organs of circulation, respiration, digestion, carry forward at a determinate rate their more humble yet necessary duties?

Such considerations teach us how visionary are the expectations of those who hope to produce, either by legal enactments or the artificial operation of education, an equality among the constituent parts of the social organism. In the body of man all is not for intellection, all is not for nutrition or assimilation—there is a diversity of duties, which, for perfection, must be harmoniously blended. And so in society, which is a vast individual—a great living, feeling, thinking mass—if its development is to go on to the utmost perfection, there must be a similar subordination of office implying a subordination of parts. Some, and by far the larger portion, must devote themselves to duties of a wholly material nature; in this representing those particles which, in the Individual, discharge the humbler offices of organic life, and provide for the nutrition and development of the body; some, on the other hand, and these relatively but few in number, are more immediately connected with the higher functions—the operations of intellect. Of these it is the especial, the unavoidable duty to exercise a direct influence over all. In China, where this principle is recognized in practical politics, they deride Occidental democracy, and consider us as hardly emerged from a barbarous state, who commit governing power to those who are altogether animalized, and can neither read nor write, instead of making intellectual power a measure of political control, as is the case in their system of statesmanship, which, on a comparatively small geographical surface, governs dense masses of men.

A closer examination of the relations of the constituent particles of the body indicates to us that they are capable of a twofold division, each having connections of an interior kind, which, as it were, concern itself alone, and also others of an exterior kind, which it maintains with the whole organism. In a metaphorical manner we may thus say that it has private and public engagements; and, considering the matter critically, we can not fail to detect that the former are essentially of a lower kind: they are indeed subordinate to the latter, for the sake of which they in reality exist. Transferring our thoughts in this particular from the individual body to the body politic, we see how great a mistake we commonly make in our appreciation of such relations. In the individual how plausibly we magnify the importance of private life, and diminish the value of the public connection! Yet it is for the latter, not for the former, that a person is brought into existence. He will have done well if, in those general relations, he has rightly discharged his duty; nor can any excellence in the private conduct compensate for any deficiency in the public. Too often we invert the sentiment on the value of which I am here insisting, and gratify a vain selfishness by concluding that we have been brought into the world each for the sake of himself; that our continuance here is for our own individual benefit; and all our hopes and aspirations for the future are restricted to ourselves, others participating therein only in an incidental and indirect way. From this narrow view we may be justly startled by a right sense of our obligations to the body of which we constitute a part, and, by a philosophical examination of our true position, learn how great a deception we are practicing upon ourselves; that we have not been introduced here and do not continue here for our own personal sake, but that we may share in the development and accomplishment of a result of a far higher order. In this the part we have to play may be, in one sense, insignificant and transient, but, in a truer sense, it is important and enduring.

We may now apply the general principles indicated on the preceding pages to the special case of America.

One of the greatest of the Greek philosophers, Plato, held that in a political sense men are to be considered, not as men, but as elements of the state; thus carrying to its extreme consequence the idea of that public relation just referred to. In America, the principle of individual independence being thoroughly admitted, that independence can only be secured by political organization; and hence, the Platonic idea being accepted, individuals must be considered as existing for the state. To it they owe whatever they have, even life.

The fabric of the Republic arose from the spontaneous coalescence of such elements. The first immigrants necessarily maintained purely democratic relations, with only such subordination as their existing needs required. When, in the course of time, colony began to establish connections with colony, the principle of equality was never for a moment forgotten. From the union of individuals towns arose; from the union of towns, states; from the union of states, the Republic. This coalescence of individuals was and is still greatly facilitated by a certain sameness of habits among all classes, arising from their issuing from a common origin. Temporary differences of wealth are of little moment: the poor of to-day may be the rich of to-morrow.

The modes of life of various classes being more similar than in Europe, individuals fall more readily into place, and more easily assume a fitting association with one another. From this arises that sentiment of equality which curbs and checks the sentiment of individual independence.

The Republic may therefore be regarded as a restrained association of free individuals, voluntarily surrendering a part of their personal independence for the common good, yet all the time conscious and jealous of that surrender. They have bartered a portion of their liberty for security. Labor is its essential basis. In America, every one, even though he may be rich, must have some ostensible occupation. A healthy public sentiment makes it disreputable to be idle.

Liberty, therefore, is always, if such a paradox may be excused, liberty under restraint. It appertains not to the position an individual occupies, it is inherent in humanity.

Elsewhere nations are governed too much; here no restraint is admissible beyond that necessary for the well-being and life of the body politic. But in that maxim much is embraced. Coercion, more energetic and more formidable than that ever felt in the most absolute monarchies, becomes justifiable, if necessary to preserve the national life. The individual must not for an instant stand in the way of the public good.

There are singular advantages arising from a personal acknowledgment of this force of public authority, and of the inevitable direction its action will take. In foreign countries there is no definitely visible path in which it is clear that the nation will advance; here every one sees plainly what the course of progress must inevitably be. The popular phrase, "manifest destiny," marks out this recognition. There hence arises a concert of action, which adds prodigiously to the public power. The momentum of the whole population is felt in a definite direction.

Placed in such circumstances, a democracy will exhibit an instinct of cohesion in all its parts. Herein is the explanation of the remark so often made by observing statesmen respecting the essential difference between democracies in Europe and America—that the former are destructive, the latter constructive.

This constructiveness is strikingly seen in new-settled American states. Where, but a short time before, there was an untrodden wilderness, population began to converge—a village formed. In an incredibly short time, organization of the infant community might be observed; its outward signs, the school-house, the town-hall, the church, the newspaper. These differentiations from the growing body spontaneously issued from the people; they required no stimulus from above. The village rapidly grew into a town. All round it, in precisely like manner, other towns were emerging. The instinct of cohesion I have referred to combined them together; an organized territory, a state, is the result. Constructive affinity still continues to be manifested, and the new state merges into and becomes an acknowledged part of the Republic. It loses forever, if indeed it ever possessed, the attribute of independent sovereignty.

Throughout this process of events self-government is perpetually manifest. Each individual bears a conscious share in each of the stages of procedure and in the final result. Hence arises a property of such a democracy unfortunately not understood in Europe. In monarchical countries war and peace are easily made. The people are rarely penetrated by a just appreciation of the points in dispute. The conflicting authorities, sovereigns or royal houses, compose their quarrel; the community acquiesces.

Not so in a self-conscious democracy. A public injury, perpetrated by a foreign power, is at once accepted by each individual as his personal affair. When the English government conceded belligerent rights to the insurgent states, there was not an American who did not personally appropriate the offense. Such a sensitiveness is often imputed, by those who have not considered the peculiarities of democratic life, to the youth of the nation or to other transitory causes. It arises, however, from a very different, and, it may be added, a far more dangerous condition. A course that might be pursued with impunity by one royal house toward another, can not wisely be pursued toward a self-conscious democracy; for it has a retentive memory, and is, in virtue of its very constitution, unforgiving.

The instinct of self-government, so characteristic of the American democracy, thus leads to the formation of villages, towns, counties, territories, states — nay, even to the expansion of the Republic itself. So far from centralization and self-government standing in opposition to each other, as some authors have supposed, the former necessarily issues out of the latter. Self-government, instead of conveying the idea of absolute freedom, conveys, in reality, the idea of restraint—restraint spontaneously imposed. If, as must be the case in self-conscious communities, that restraint is organized by those who are intending to submit to its rule, centralization is the necessary result.

Moreover, the instinct of self-government implies an instinct for enlightenment — an insatiable thirst for information. This is recognized in all directions in America. It satisfies itself by the creation of great educational establishments, and descends even to amusing details. The Yankee converses in questions.

Every one is penetrated with the conviction that for social advancement to pursue the right direction, and to be pressed forward at the highest speed, it must be controlled by intelligence. Hence the public prosperity is considered to depend on education. There can be no doubt that this is a very high and noble conception. It establishes an intrinsic difference between the people of Europe and the people of America.

In Europe the attempt has been made to govern communities through their morals alone. The present state of that continent, at the close of so many centuries, shows how great the failure has been. In America, on the contrary, the attempt is to govern through intelligence. It will succeed.

From the American principle, it follows that whoever seeks the improvement of his fellow-men, the ennobling of the community among whom he lives, or the true glory of the nation, can best accomplish his purpose by spreading forth the light of knowledge, and strengthening and developing the public understanding.

For more than a thousand years the moral system has been tried in Europe. Its agent, the ecclesiastic, was animated by intentions that were good, by perseverance unwearied, by a vigorous energy. The failure is attributable, not to shortcomings in him, but to intrinsic defects in his method; though on that continent, in a very imperfect manner, in later times the other method has spontaneously and with much resistance made itself felt; a wonderful result is beginning to be apparent. The apprehension entertained by many good men in former times, that if the mind be instructed the morals may be injured, has proved to be unfounded. Men are better in proportion as they are wiser. In whatever direction we look, we see the improvement. The physical man is more powerful, the intellectual man more perfect, the moral man more pure. For the poor, in the midst of all this social activity, this business energy, charity is none the less overflowing; for him who wishes to improve his life there is certain to be encouragement.

Whoever in America desires to better his fellowmen must act by influencing their intellect. If he wishes to see no idle man and no poor man in the land, he must take care that there shall be no ignorant man. Ignorance is not, as in the old times they used to say, the mother of devotion; she is the mother of superstition and misery.

If we wish to know how we may best clear from this continent the superabundant forests that encumber it—how we may best lay the iron rail and put the locomotive upon it—how we may most profitably dig the abounding metals from their veins—how we may instantaneously communicate with our most distant towns—how we may cover the ocean with our ships—how we may produce a sober, industrious, healthy, moral population, we shall find our answer in providing universal instruction. That spontaneously provides occupation. The morality of a nation is the aggregate of the morality of individuals. A lazy man is necessarily a bad man; an idle is necessarily a demoralized population.

In such provisions for the rising generations there is a special interest which ought never to be overlooked. On many occasions social requirements press with melancholy severity on the female sex. Women can not engage in the rough conflicts of life. Few are the occupations to which they can with propriety turn, and even in those few, to the disgrace of men be it said, they are jostled, and crushed, and crowded out. Yet often the friendless woman has duties to perform for herself and those dependent on her of the highest kind. Society inexorably binds her with all its rules and usages, yet society too often yields her but a feeble help. No more is wanted than freedom for her hands, no more than opportunity, yet how often is that freedom, that opportunity denied! How many of the fearful evils of great cities may be directly traced to the compulsory, the profitless inaction of young women!

I repeat again the great truth, that the only method of ameliorating the condition of men is by acting on their intelligence; even their morals must be guided by their understanding. This principle has been carried into practical effect by a race whom we affect to despise. Ages ago, in China, they had passed through the various experiments which the Western nations are now so sedulously trying; and ages ago they came to the conclusion that government, to be effectual, satisfactory, permanent, must operate through the public intelligence. In that they follow nature. In our supercilious conceit we laugh at the Chinese; his bodily formation and grotesque manners are topics of merriment to us. We say he opens his eyes vertically, like a pair of folding doors, our own opening horizontally, as properly fixed windows ought to do. We exult in the glory of a luxuriant beard spread broadly over the breast, and ridicule him who, having none, ties up his long hair into a tail, and lets it hang down his back. But the wisdom of a man does not depend on these decorations being either in front or behind. If we, knowing very imperfectly the ideas of the old man of the Mongols, irreverently set him down as a superannuated dotard, he, in an equally imperfect way, learning of our proceedings in statecraft and our anarchy of creeds, regards us as "outside barbarians," and, judging from the rude violence with which we seek to make him recognize our acquaintance, as "red-headed devils."

But this supremely solemn old man has done something that we can not help seeing, no matter in what way we open our eyes. He has found out the means by which more than three hundred millions of men

—more than ten times the population of the United States—more than one third of the human race, have been for ages kept in happiness, prosperity, and peace. Long ago he had accomplished the thing which we, on a smaller scale, are attempting. If we could surprise him into a moment's relaxation from the amenities of exquisite courteousness and from the artifices of infinite dissimulation—if we could coax from him his secret, this is what he would say: "Educate every body. In every child that is born, the state, as well as the parent, has a right. I compel all to go to school. I push forward the brightest of the children into academies, and from thence the boys who are distinguished above their fellow-boys by superior endowments I send to the college. From the new conflict of mind that there ensues I select the victors, and, transplanting them to active life, intrust to them the superintendence of districts. Those who have displayed capacity on that scale I promote to the government of provinces. They who approve themselves in the ordeal of that greater trial are relied upon as the counselors and guides of the Imperial authority at last. In China our ancestors organized the National Intellect; we honor learning above all other things. The road to greatness is open to him who has capacity to walk in it. Our educated are not our dangerous classes, but firm supporters of the state; and the result is, that we are the most numerous, in our internal affairs the most prosperous and the most contented nation of the earth."

That is the manner in which the Asiatics have resolved the great problem of statesmanship. The details might not answer to our Western life, but their example and its success may well afford us a topic of profound meditation.

It is not necessary here to discuss formally the question whether social advancement is best secured through moral or intellectual action. In America the latter method has been adopted; and accepting that in contradistinction to the former, which is followed in Europe, I may briefly allude to certain points connected with the practical manner in which it is carried into effect.

There are three organs of public instruction—the school, the pulpit, the press.

As respects schools, the primary condition for their efficiency is a supply of well-trained and competent teachers. In former times the education of youth was too often surrendered to persons who had become superannuated in other pursuits, or had failed in them, or had been left in destitute circumstances. But little heed was given by parents or the public to the quality of the information imparted in these concerns. There was a vague notion, which, as we shall see, still unhappily prevails as regards the higher establishments of education, that the training of the mind is of more importance than the nature of the information imparted to it.

Normal schools for the preparation of teachers must necessarily be an essential part of any well-ordered public school system. In these, young persons of both sexes may be prepared for assuming the duties of teaching. The rule under which they should not only be taught, but likewise subsequently teach—the rule that should be made to apply in every establishment, from the primary school to the university, is this—Education should represent the existing state of knowledge.

But in America this golden rule is disregarded, especially in the case of the higher establishments. What is termed classical learning arrogates to itself a space that excludes much more important things. It finds means to appropriate, practically, all collegiate honors. This evil has arisen from the circumstance that our system was imported from England. It is a remnant of the tone of thought of that country in the sixteenth century; meritorious enough and justifiable enough in that day, but obsolete in this. The vague impression to which I have above referred, that such pursuits impart a training to the mind, has long sustained this inappropriate course. It also finds an excuse in its alleged power of communicating the wisdom of past ages. The grand depositories of human knowledge are not the ancient, but the modern tongues. Few, if any, are the facts worth knowing that are to be exclusively obtained by a knowledge of Latin and Greek; and as to mental discipline, it might reasonably be inquired how much a youth will secure by translating daily a few good sentences of Latin and Greek into bad and broken English. So far as a preparation is required for the subsequent struggles and conflicts of life—for discerning the intentions and meeting the rivalries of competitors—for skill to design movements and carry them out with success—for cultivating a clearness of perception into the character and motives of others, and for imparting a decision to our own actions—so far as these things are concerned, an ingenious man would have no difficulty in maintaining the amusing affirmation that more might be gained from a mastery of the game of chess than by translating all the Greek and Latin authors in the world.

The remarks I am thus making respecting the imperfections of general education apply, I think, very forcibly to the education of the clergy. The school, the pulpit, the press, being the three organs of public instruction, a right preparation of the clergy for their duty is of as much moment as a right preparation of teachers and journalists.

In the education of the American clergyman the classical element very largely predominates. Indeed, it may with truth be affirmed that it is to no inconsiderable degree for the sake of securing such a result that that element is so carefully fostered in the colleges, from which it would otherwise have long ago been eliminated, or, at all events, greatly reduced in prominence. The strength of this wish is manifested by the munificent endowments with which many pious and patriotic men have sustained classical professorships. Perhaps, however, they do not sufficiently reflect that the position and requirements of the clergy have of late years very much changed. Preaching must answer to the mode of thinking of the congregations. But now literary authority has to a very great degree lost its force. Elucidations of Scripture and the defense of doctrine, in modern times, require modern modes of treatment.

But, moreover, in one important respect is the education of the clergy defective. Unhappily, and, it may be added, unnecessarily, there has arisen, as was related in the last chapter, an apparent antagonism between Theology and Science. Tradition has been made to confront Discovery. Now, the discussion and correct appreciation of any new scientific fact requires a special training, a special stock of knowledge. That training, that knowledge, are not to be had in theological seminaries. The clergyman is thus constrained to view with jealous distrust the rapid advancement of practical knowledge. In the case of any new fact, his inquiry necessarily is, not whether it is absolutely true, but whether it is in accordance with conceptions he considers established. The result of this condition of things is, that many of the most important, the most powerful and exact branches of human knowledge, have been forced into a position they never would have voluntarily assumed, and have been compelled to put themselves on their defense—Astronomy, in the case of the globular form of the earth, and its position as a subordinate planet; Geology, as respects its vast antiquity; Zoology, on the problem of the origin of species; Chemistry, on the unchangeability of matter and the indestructibility of force.

In thus criticising education in the higher American establishments, I present views that have forced themselves on my attention in an experience of thirty years, and on a very extensive scale. Not unfrequently I have superintended the instruction, professional or otherwise, of nearly four hundred young men in the course of a single year, and have had unusual opportunities of observing their subsequent course of life.

The education of the clergy, I think, is not equal to that of physicians or lawyers. The provisions are sufficient, and the time is sufficient, but the direction is faulty. In the study of medicine every thing is done to impart to the pupil a knowledge of the present state of the subjects or sciences with which he is concerned. The profession watches with a jealous eye its colleges, exposing without hesitation any shortcomings it detects. It will not be satisfied with erudition, it insists on knowledge.

But such modernized instruction is actually less necessary in the life of a physician than it is in the life of a clergyman. The former pursues his daily course in an unobtrusive way; the latter is compelled by his position to publicity. The congregations whom he must meet each Sabbath day, and, indeed, perhaps more frequently, are often too prone to substitute the right of criticism for a sentiment of simple devotion. Very few among them can appreciate the monotonous, the wearing strain of compulsory mental labor—labor that at a given hour must with punctuality be performed. On topics that have been thought about, and written about, and preached about for nearly twenty centuries, they are importunately and unreasonably demanding something new.

In that ordeal the clergyman spends his existence. To maintain the respect that is his due, there are but two things on which he can rely—purity of life and knowledge. Men unconsciously submit to the guidance of what they discern to be superior intelligence. Here comes into disastrous operation the defective organization of the theological seminaries. Content with such a knowledge of nature as might have answered a century ago, the imposing and ever-increasing body of modern science they decline. And yet it is that science and its practical applications which are now guiding the destinies of civilization.

In my History of the Intellectual Development of Europe I have had occasion to consider the consequences of the Reformation, and may perhaps be excused the following quotation: "America, in which, of all countries, the Reformation at the present moment has farthest advanced, should offer to thoughtful men much encouragement. Its cities are filled with churches built by voluntary gifts; its clergy are voluntarily sustained, and are in all directions engaged in enterprises of piety, education, mercy. What a difference between their private life and that of ecclesiastics before the Reformation! Not, as in the old times, does the layman look upon them as the cormorants and curse of society. They are his faithful advisers, his honored friends, under whose suggestion and supervision are instituted educational establishments, colleges, hospitals, whatever can be of benefit to men in this life, or secure for them happiness in the life to come."

No one can study the progress of modern civilization without being continually reminded of the great, it might be said, the mortal mistake committed by the Roman Church. Had it put itself forth as the promoter and protector of science, it would at this day have exerted an unquestioned dominion all over

Europe. Instead of being the stumbling-block, it would have been the animating agent of human advancement. It shut the Bible only to have it opened forcibly by the Reformation; it shut the book of Nature, but has found it impossible to keep it closed. How different the result, had it abandoned the obsolete absurdities of Patristicism, and become imbued with the spirit of true Philosophy—had it lifted itself to a comprehension of the awful magnificence of the heavens above and the glories of the earth beneath—had it appreciated the immeasurable vastness of the universe, its infinite multitude of worlds, its inconceivable past duration! How different, if in place of forever looking backward, it had only looked forward—bowing itself down in a world of life and light, instead of worshiping, in the charnel-house of antiquity, the skeletons of twenty centuries! How different, had it hailed with transport the discoveries and inventions of human genius, instead of scowling upon them with a malignant and baleful eye! How different, had it canonized the great men who have been the interpreters of Nature, instead of anathematizing them as Atheists!

In our national development it is for the American clergy to shun that great, that fatal mistake. It is for them to remember that the Reformation remains only half completed, until to the free reading of the Book of God there is added the free reading of the

Book of Nature. It is for them to remember that there are two volumes of Revelation—the Word and the Works; and that it is the indefeasible right of every man to study and interpret them both, according to the light given him, without molestation or punishment.

Since the invention of printing, the power of the pulpit has been subordinated to the power of the press, which is continually gathering force from the increasing diffusion of education. In America the newspaper has become a necessary of life. It makes its successful appearance in villages of which the population would be considered, in other countries, inadequate for its support. Cheap reading is to be had every where. The consequence is, that all sides of a question are apt to be read. It is affirmed that the consumption of paper in America, for printing and writing, is more than that of England and France put together.

By these various agencies rays of enlightenment pervade the land; the general character of the people undergoing a continual improvement, manifested in the acquisition of a breadth of view and vigor of action. It is both important and interesting to compare communities whose improvement has been attempted on the moral principle alone, with the American community, in which dependence is had on the intellectual. The people who approach most nearly to us, so far as origin and habits of life are concerned, are the English. For many centuries their social amelioration and political advancement were dependent on an appeal to morals. During the greater portion of that time the country had been Catholic, but then it had also been reformed—ever, as it will always be, religious. In my History of the Intellectual Development of Europe, Chapter XXI., I have endeavored to estimate impartially the progress that had been made under that system, and to give a picture of the social state attained by its guidance. I think that any one who will turn to those pages will come to the conclusion that, even when thus perseveringly applied for many ages, under auspices of the most favorable and varied kind, upon a people naturally desirous of improvement, the moral method fails to yield the results popularly imputed to it.

No social problem can be presented to our contemplation of higher importance. Shall we decide in favor of the moral or the intellectual method? the English or the American system? For the sake of enabling the reader to judge, I will present a brief abstract of some of the facts set forth in the chapter to which I have alluded. They are derived altogether from English sources, and to a considerable extent from the works of Lord Macaulay and Mr. Froude.

At the close of the seventeenth century London was the most populous capital in Europe; yet it was dirty, ill built, without sanitary provisions. The deaths were one in twenty-three each year; now, in a much more crowded population, they are not one in forty. Much of the country was heath, swamp, warren. Almost within sight of the city there was a tract twenty-five miles round nearly in a state of nature; there were but three houses upon it. Wild animals roamed in all directions.

Nothing more strikingly shows the social condition than the provisions for locomotion. In the rainy seasons the roads were all but impassable, justifying the epithet so often applied to them of being in a horrible state. Through such gullies, half filled with mud, carriages were dragged, often by oxen, or, when horses were used, it was as much a matter of necessity as, in the city, a matter of display, to drive half a dozen of them. If the country was open, the track of the road was easily mistaken: it was no uncommon thing for persons to lose their way, and have to spend the night out in the open air. Between places of considerable importance the roads were very little known; and such was the difficulty for wheeled carriages, that a principal mode of transport was by pack-horses, of which the passengers took advantage, stowing themselves away between the packs. We shall probably not dissent from their complaint that this method of traveling was hot in summer and cold in winter. The usual charge for freight was thirty cents a ton per mile. Toward the close of the century, what were termed flying coaches were established: they could move at the rate of from thirty to fifty miles a day. Many persons thought the risk so great that it was a tempting of Providence to go in them. The mail-bag was carried on horseback at about five miles an hour. A penny-post had been established in the city, but with much difficulty; for many long-headed men, who knew very well what they were saying, had denounced it as an insidious "Popish contrivance."

Only a few years before this period Parliament had resolved that "all pictures in the royal collection which contained representations of Jesus or the Virgin Mother should be burned. Greek statues were delivered over to Puritan stone-masons to be made decent." A little earlier, Lewis Muggleton had given himself out as the last and greatest of the prophets, having power to save or damn whom he pleased. It had been revealed to him that God is only six feet high, and the sun only four miles off. The country beyond the Trent was still in a state of barbarism, and near the sources of the Tyne there were people scarcely less savage than American Indians, their "half-naked women chanting a wild measure, while the men, with brandished dirks, danced a war-dance."

At the beginning of the eighteenth century there were thirty-four counties without a printer. The only press in England north of the Trent was at

York. As to private libraries, there were none deserving the name. "An esquire passed for a great scholar, if Hudibras, Baker's Chronicle, Tarleton's Jests, and the Seven Champions of Christendom lay in his hall window." It might be expected that the women were ignorant enough, when very few men knew how to write correctly or even intelligibly, and it had become unnecessary for clergymen to read the Scriptures in the original tongues.

Social discipline was very far from being of that kind which we call moral. The master whipped his apprentice, the pedagogue his scholar, the husband his wife. Public punishments partook of the general brutality. It was a day for the rabble when a culprit was set in the pillory, to be pelted with brickbats, rotten eggs, and dead cats; when women were fastened by the legs in the stocks at the market-place, or a pilferer flogged through the town at the cart tail, a clamor not unfrequently arising unless the lash were laid on hard enough "to make him howl." In punishments of a higher kind these whippings were perfectly horrible: thus Titus Oates, after standing twice in the pillory, was whipped, and, after an interval of a few days, whipped again. A virtuoso in these matters gives us the incredible information that he counted as many as seventeen hundred stripes administered. So far from the community being shocked at such an exhibition, they appeared to agree in the sentiment, that "since his face could not be made to blush, it was well enough to try what could be done with his back." Such a hardening of heart was in no little degree promoted by the atrocious punishment of state offenders; thus, after the decapitation of Montrose and Argyle, their heads decorated the top of the Tolbooth; and gentlemen, after the rising of Monmouth, were admonished to be careful of their ways, by hanging in chains to their park gate the corpse of a rebel to rot in the air.

To a debased public life private life corresponded. The houses of the rural population were huts covered with straw thatch; their inmates, if able to procure fresh meat once a week, were considered to be in prosperous circumstances; one half of the families in England could hardly do that. Children of six years old were not unfrequently set to labor. The lord of the manor spent his time in rustic pursuits, was not an unwilling associate of peddlers and drovers, knew how to ring a pig or shoe a horse; his wife and daughters "stitched and spun, brewed gooseberry wine, cured marigolds, and made the crust for the venison pasty." Hospitality was displayed in immoderate eating and the drinking of beer, the guest not being considered as having done justice to the occasion unless he had gone under the table. The dining-room was uncarpeted, but then it was tinted with a decoction of "soot and small beer." The chairs were rush-bottomed. In

London the houses were mostly of wood and plaster, the streets filthy beyond expression. After nightfall a passenger went at his peril, for chamber windows were opened and slop-pails unceremoniously emptied down. There were no lamps in the streets until Master Fleming established his public lanterns. As a necessary consequence, there were plenty of shoplifters, highwaymen, and burglars.

As to the moral condition, it is fearfully expressed in the statement that men not unfrequently were willing to sacrifice their country for their religion. Hardly any person died who was not suspected to have been made away with by poison, an indication of the morality generally supposed to prevail among the higher classes. If such was the state of society in its serious aspect, it was no better in its lighter. We can scarcely credit the impurity and immodesty of the theatrical exhibitions. What is said about them would be beyond belief, if we did not remember that they were the amusements of a community whose ideas of female modesty and female sentiment were altogether different from ours. Indecent jests were put into the mouths of lively actresses, and the dancing was not altogether of a kind to meet our approval. The rural clergy could do but little to withstand this flood of immorality. Their social condition for the last hundred years had been rapidly declining; for, though the Church possessed among her dignitaries great writers and great preachers, her lower orders, partly through the political troubles that had befallen the state, but chiefly in consequence of sectarian bitterness, had been reduced to a truly menial condition. It was the business of the rich man's chaplain to add dignity to the dinner-table by saying grace "in full canonicals," but he was also intended to be a butt for the mirth of the company. "The young Levite," such was the phrase then in use, "might fill himself with the corned beef and the carrots; but, as soon as the tarts and cheesecakes made their appearance, he quitted his seat and stood aloof till he was summoned to return thanks for the repast," the daintiest part of which he had not tasted. If need arose, he could curry a horse, "carry a parcel ten miles," or "cast up the farrier's bill." The "wages" of a parish priest were at starvation-point. The social degradation of the ecclesiastics is well illustrated by an order of Queen Elizabeth, that no clergyman should presume to marry a servant-girl without the consent of her master or mistress.

In administering the law, whether in relation to political or religious offenses, there was an incredible atrocity. In London, the crazy old bridge over the Thames was decorated with grinning and mouldering heads of criminals, under an idea that these ghastly spectacles would fortify the common people in their resolves to act according to law. The toleration of the times may be understood from a law enacted by the Scotch Parliament, May 8, 1685, that whoever preached or heard in a conventicle should be punished with death and the confiscation of his goods. That such an infamous spirit should not content itself with mere dead-letter laws, there is too much practical evidence to permit any one to doubt. A silly laboring man, who had taken it into his head that he could not conscientiously attend the Episcopal worship, was seized by a troop of soldiers, "rapidly examined, convicted of nonconformity, and sentenced to death in the presence of his wife, who led one little child by the hand, and, it was easy to see, was about to give birth to another. He was shot before her face, the widow crying out, in her agony, 'Well, sirs, well, the day of reckoning will come.'" Shrieking Scotch Covenanters were submitted to torture by crushing their knees flat in the boot. Women were tied to stakes on the sea-sands and drowned by the slowly advancing tide because they would not attend Episcopal worship, or branded on their cheeks and then shipped to America. Gallant but wounded soldiers were hung in Scotland, for fear they should die before they could be got to England. In the troubles connected with Monmouth's rising, in one county alone, Somersetshire, two hundred and thirty-three persons were hanged, drawn, and quartered, to say nothing of military executions; for the soldiers amused themselves by hanging a culprit for each toast they drank, and making the drums and fifes play, as they said, to his dancing. It is needless to recall such incidents as the ferocity of Kirk's lambs, for such was the name popularly given to the soldiers of that colonel, in allusion to the Paschal Lamb they bore on their flag, or to the story of Tom Boilman, so nicknamed from his having been compelled by those veterans to seethe the remains of his quartered friends in melted pitch. Women, for such idle words as women are always using, were sentenced to be whipped at the cart's tail through every market-town in Dorset. A lad named Tutching was condemned to be flogged once a fortnight for seven years. Eight hundred and forty-one human beings, judicially condemned to transportation to the West India Islands, and suffering all the horrible pains of a slave-ship in the Middle Passage, "were never suffered to go on deck;" in the holds below, "all was darkness, stench, lamentation, disease, and death." One fifth of them were thrown overboard to the sharks before they reached their destination, and the rest obliged to be fattened before they could be offered in the market to the Jamaica planters. The court ladies, and even the queen herself, were so utterly forgetful of womanly mercy and common humanity as to join in this infernal traffic. That princess requested that a hundred of the convicts should be given to her. "The profit which she cleared on the cargo, after making a large allowance for those who died of hunger and fever during the passage, can not be estimated at less than a thousand guineas."

Such incidents as that last mentioned would be incredible, if not cited upon unimpeachable authority. It is that of Lord Macaulay, in his History of England. The advocates of the system of social improvement by an appeal to the moral, excluding the intellectual, have in this impartial representation of the state of that country, after a persevering trial of hundreds of years of that means, a proof of the failure of their well-meant but inadequate work.

Why is it that such things are impossible now? The answer promptly given to such an inquiry is, that men are more enlightened. Exactly so. And does not that confession concede the principle I am endeavoring to enforce, that the improvement of society can only be accomplished through the intellect?

The moral is, in its very nature, stationary. Alone it is incompetent to guide the advancement of society. Social elevation can only be accomplished by appealing to the understanding, and that will influence the heart.

Herein is the secret of the rapid development of American society, and the prodigious strength of American political institutions. If education were restricted to a class, instead of being given to all, the dead weight of the illiterate masses would keep every thing in stagnation.

Whoever will examine the social condition of Europe from the epoch of its conversion to the close of the seventeenth century, will not fail to perceive that its torpidity through so many ages was connected with the false system resorted to by the Italian authorities. Rome utterly rejected intellectual improvement; she struck it aside with an inexorable, often with a bloody hand. She fell into the political error of expecting to accomplish the development of society by methods that were essentially inadequate and stationary.

"Ignorance is the mother of Devotion"—of Superstition, it should rather have been said. There can not be found in any country communities more religious and more enlightened than American. Knowledge and morality, so far from being incompatible, are intimately allied. Whatever improvement the latter is capable of, it must owe to the advancement of the former.

It is amazing what delusions and impostures held an unquestioned position so long as that erroneous system was applied. It is amazing how they disappeared when the better system was put in force. The moonlight has now no fairies, the solitude no genius, the darkness no ghost, no goblin. There is no necromancer who can raise the dead from their graves,

—no one who has sold his soul to the devil and signed the contract with his blood—no angry apparition to rebuke the crone who has disquieted him. Divination, agromancy, pyromancy, hydromancy, cheiromancy, augury, interpreting of dreams, oracles, sorcery, astrology, are all gone. It is three hundred and fifty years since the last sepulchral lamp was found, and that was near Rome. There are no gorgons, hydras, chimeras, no familiars, no incubus or succubus. No longer do captains buy of Lapland witches favorable winds; no longer do our churches resound with prayers against the baleful influences of comets, though there still linger in some of our noble old rituals forms of supplication for dry weather and rain—useless but not unpleasing reminiscences of the past. The apothecary no longer says prayers over the mortar in which he is pounding, to impart a divine afflatus to his drugs. Who is there that now pays fees to a relic, or goes to a saint shrine to be cured? These delusions have vanished, together with the night to which they appertained, yet they were the delusions of fifteen hundred years. In their support might be produced a greater mass of human testimony than probably could be brought to bear on any other matter of belief in the entire history of man; and yet in the nineteenth century we have come to the conclusion that the whole, from the beginning to the end, was a deception. Let him, therefore, who is disposed to balance the testimony of past ages against the dictates of his own reason ponder on this strange history. Let him who relies on the authority of human evidence in the guidance of his opinions, now settle with himself what that evidence is worth.

The value of social methods is to be determined by an ascertainment of their practical working. We have only to compare the slow progress made by Europe when under its moral education, with the rapid advancement of America under its intellectual education. How striking is the contrast between the infatuated supernaturalism of the one, and the plain common sense of the other! For many successive centuries the former was a theatre of magic. It was not until the Reformation that an end was put to those disgraceful miracles that were a public scandal. As enlightenment advanced they could no longer be made to succeed. Even Rome, the workshop of those artifices, ceased to be the seat of that trade. They could never be imposed on America.

But, though this continent rejected those impostures, it has been the scene of wonders of a very different kind—miracles not ending when the enchanter ceased waving his wand, and requiring the authentication of credible or credulous witnesses, but lasting for all time and open to all eyes. From the Atlantic shore-line to a vast distance in the interior the forests that encumbered the ground have been cut down; the gloomy waste has become fertile fields; roads for hundreds of thousands of miles have been constructed; rivers have been bridged; canals have been dug. The self-multiplying force of society has at length here found unrestrained scope; the population increases with unparalleled rapidity. A network of iron, daily increasing in extent, has been spread; telegraphic wires run in all directions. Great cities, with hundreds of thousands of inhabitants, have arisen. A large portion of Europe is fed by the harvests that are gathered; a large portion of the human race turns hither for its clothing. The people on the borders of the great lakes can speak instantaneously to those on the Gulf of Mexico; those on the Atlantic and Pacific can do the same. Innumerable churches, and colleges, and hospitals are scattered over the land in all directions. The ports are forests of masts. The flag of the country is seen on every sea and from every shore.

A self-conscious democracy has wrung from its rivals and enemies the reluctant confession that "it is not fickle to its rulers, unstable in its policy, wavering in its determination;" that "it is not violent or cruel, nor too impatient of discipline and obedience to be inapt for military success;" that "it will support the expenses of war and the burden of taxation." They speak of the opinions which Europe has held on these points as "delusions" unsafe any longer to entertain. It has also taught them the portentous lesson that "a despot is not necessary for the conducting of a great war," in which there are engaged armies of a million of men and a navy of a thousand ships.

These are a sample of the miracles that spring from Intelligence. Compare them with the miracles done in a corner—that spring from superstition. They are also the miracles of Peace.

But there are also miracles of War. In a land where every man is free to think and free to act as he likes—where one might suppose that there would, of necessity, be a Babel hubbub of confusion, and society be only a rope of sand, the shot of a gun at their flag brought half a million of riflemen into the field. The waste of battle and the hospitals was for years more than supplied. With admirable energy, an iron-clad navy, that can match the navies of the world, was sent to sea. Never was there such an exhibition of public resolution and of private charity. If an army of a hundred thousand men melted away before cannon and by fever, there was another army of a hundred and fifty thousand men put in its place. The wars of Europe, even those of the French Empire, were outdone in brilliancy and in result. The man of the Northwest hewed his way with his sword to the Gulf of Mexico by a river more than a thousand miles long, paving its bottom with the wrecks of ships. The man of the Northeast executed marches of more than two thousand miles, resistlessly capturing cities and subjugating states: there were trophies of thousands of guns. The mouth of the Mississippi was forced by one of the most brilliant operations in naval annals. The art of war, both by land and sea, was absolutely remodeled. Slavery, that, like a gnarled Upas-tree, had struck its roots into a country almost one fourth the size of Europe, was wrenched out of the earth. A track of grim desolation, of unutterable ruin, marked where the avenging cannon-wheels had passed. There were spent three thousand millions of dollars, and yet this people put off its armor more powerful, richer, better, than ever before.

Is there any miracle the Old World can show the equal of that? And what was it worked for? For the sake of an Idea—that there shall exist on this continent one Republic, great and indivisible.

Such, then, are the fruits of the culture of the Intellect, such are the advantages the American has over the European system: in truth, it belongs to a higher stage of social life. We have already seen that, in the general plan of Nature, the direction of evolution is altogether toward the intellectual; a conclusion equally impressed upon us whether our mode of examination be anatomical or historical. Anatomically we find no provision in the nervous system for the improvement of the moral, save indirectly through the intellectual, the whole aim of development being for the sake of intelligence. Historically, in the same manner, we find that the intellectual has always led the way in social advancement, the moral having been subordinate thereto. The former has been the main-spring of the movement, the latter passively affected. It is a mistake to make the progress of society depend on that which is itself controlled by a higher power. In the earlier and inferior stages of individual life we may govern through the moral alone. In that way we may guide children, but it is to the understanding of the adult that we must appeal. A system working only through the moral must, sooner or later, come into antagonism with the intellectual, and if it does not contain within itself a means of adaptation to the changing circumstances, must in the end be overthrown. This was the grand error of that Roman system which presided while European civilization was developing. It assumed as its basis a uniform, a stationary psychological condition in man. Forgetting that the powers of the mind grow with the possessions of the mind, it considered those who lived in past generations as being in no respect mentally inferior to those who are living now, though our children at sixteen may have a wider range of knowledge than our ancestors at sixty. That such an imperfect system could exist for so many ages is a proof of a contemporary condition of undeveloped intellect, as we see that the understanding of a child does not revolt against the moral suasion, often intrinsically feeble, with which we attempt to influence him. But it would be as unphilosophical to treat with disdain the ideas that have served as a guide in the earlier ages of European life, as to look with contempt on the motives that have guided us in youth. Their feebleness and incompetency are excused by their suitability to the period of life to which they are applied.

But whoever considers these things will see that there is a term beyond which the application of such methods can not be extended. The head of a family would act unwisely if he attempted to apply to his son at twenty-one the methods he had successfully used at ten: such methods could only be rendered effective by a resort to physical compulsion. A great change in the intervening years has taken place, and ideas once intrinsically powerful can exert their influence no more. The moral may have remained unchanged, it may be precisely as it was—no better, no worse; but that which has changed is the understanding. Reasoning and inducements of an intellectual kind are now needful.

If it is thus with the individual, it is likewise so with humanity. For centuries nations may live under forms that meet their requirements—forms suitable to a feeble state; but it is altogether illusory to suppose that such an adaptedness can continue forever. A critical eye discerns that the mental features of a given generation have become different from those of its ancestors. New ideas and a new manner of action are the tokens that a modification has silently taken place. Though after a short interval the change might not amount to much, in the course of time there must inevitably be exhibited the spectacle of a society that had outgrown its forms, its rules of life.

In the work from which I have so frequently quoted I have considered in detail the theme here presented, and have endeavored to show that there is a complete analogy between individual and national life. Selecting for preliminary examination the only European nation offering a complete and completed intellectual life, and out of the five general topics that might be resorted to—philosophy, science, literature, religion, government—using the first as best suited for the purpose, I have endeavored to ascertain the characteristics of Greek mental development, expecting to find that the younger members of the European family, more or less distinctly, would offer illustrations of the same mode of advancement; and that, indeed, the whole continent, which is the aggregate of these separate elements, would in its secular progress comport itself in a like way. From such an examination it appears that the whole movement in question is of a nature answering to that observed in an individual, and, like it, conveniently separable into arbitrary periods sufficiently distinct from one another. In succession there may be observed an age of credulity, an age of inquiry, an age of faith, an age of reason, an age of decrepitude. The first, the age of credulity, which had filled the Mediterranean Sea with monsters and marvels, was closed by geographical discovery; the second, which includes the Ionian, the Pythagorean, the Eleatic philosophies, was ended by the criticisms of the Sophists; the third, embracing the Socratic and Platonic, by the doubts of the Skeptics; the fourth, ushered in by the Macedonian expedition in a material sense, and in a philosophical by Aristotle and the Stoics, and adorned by the splendid achievements of the Alexandrian school, degenerated into imbecility, Neo-platonism, and mysticism; and the hand of Rome put an end to the fifth. In the mental progress of this people we therefore discern the forthshadowing of a career like that of individual life—a career of which the epochs answer to those of infancy, childhood, youth, manhood, old age.

Is there not a wide step from the simple, and, indeed, childlike inquiries of the Ionians as to the primary element, to the majestic speculations and abiding faith of Platonism, and another to that exact science which culminated in the Museum of Alexandria, and still another to the superstition of Plotinus? The strong man of Stoicism had degenerated into the superannuated dotard, full of admiration for the past, of contemptuous disgust for the present, his thoughts wandering back to the things that had occupied him in his youth and even in his infancy. In this its closing scene, Greek philosophy is garrulity and mysticism.

From the solution of the four great problems of Greek philosophy given in each of the five stages of its life, it is not difficult to determine the law of the variation of Greek opinion, and to show its analogy to that of the variation of the opinions in individual life. A supreme interest gathers round such an analysis when we compare what was here accomplished with what had been done in the same direction by the ancestry of the Indo-Germanic nations in Asia; when we see emerging in Europe, spontaneously or willingly adopted, the majestic ideas of India, where man had risen to the grand conception of a multiplicity of worlds in infinite space, and a succession of worlds in infinite time.

And now it may be clearly shown that these phases of Greek intellect are already in part repeated in the life of Europe, though it is a continent of many meteorological contrasts, and has a varied surface of relief, and is therefore full of modified men. For it, too, there have been successive ages. An age of credulity, the old Pagan times, was ended by the spread of the power of republican Rome; a period then intervenes up to the foundation of Constantinople—it is one of inquiry; then follows an age of faith, the Turkish invasion of Europe marking its close. The harbingers of the age of reason were maritime discovery and philosophical criticism; the former being still more effective in its operation than in ancient times, for it dislocated the centre of material activity and the centre of intellect, changing the front of Europe from the north shore of the Mediterranean Sea to the Atlantic Ocean, and forced nations that had hitherto lain eccentrically and in comparative obscurity into the very van of the new movement.

This regular advance of Europe toward its age of reason was to no small extent affected by two agencies, to which it would appear that sufficient importance has not yet been attached. The first of these was altogether scientific; it was the influence of the Jewish physicians. Its range is over a period of more than seven centuries. The second, the Arabian action, was partly intellectual and partly political. Of all the incidents of European life, this is the most misunderstood and undervalued.

From the age that could accept without question the scientific ideas of patristicism, to that which delighted in the abstruse metaphysics of Abelard, there is a very great step; there is also another very great one before we reach the age of Newton. At intermediate periods, a much shorter space apart, the variations in the movement are so distinct, and their general tendency so obvious, that for an observing man to have overlooked them seems almost an impossibility. To assert that the earth is stationary is a much less surprising error than to assert the mental immobility of man; yet it is very well known that even so lately as the seventeenth century this doctrine was the basis of the European political system.

This gradual process of intellectual development, shown so strikingly by the past history of Europe, so strikingly in its present life, is destined, necessarily, likewise to be shown by America;

> "For, I doubt not, through the ages an increasing purpose runs,
> And the thoughts of men are widened by the process of the suns."

Here the direction of the movement is altogether toward the intellectual. The advance is so rapid, the consequent material results are so prodigious, that they seem more like the castle-building of a wild romancer than the calculated realities of a political economist.

From that intellectual aspect which in so marked a manner it is fast assuming, it is plain that this continent is destined for ages to be the seat of a conflict of ideas.

The law of action and reaction obtains as completely in the collisions of human opinion as in the mechanical collisions of bodies. An idea can not make its way through nations without receiving from them a special impress, and becoming modified by the ideas it encounters. Whatever may be its innate force, whatever its massiveness, it is influenced by them in proportion to their firmness or their power.

Such is undoubtedly the true effect, but very often it assumes a deceptive aspect. When a stone falls to the earth, the earth rises through a definite distance to meet the stone, and the amount of motion accomplished by each is capable of an exact scientific determination; but, considering the relative masses of the two bodies, we may, for all practical purposes, without sensible error, neglect the movement of the greater, and consider the descending stone as alone affected.

So with an Idea: its massiveness and its momentum may long preserve it without sensible modification. For practical purposes, it, too, may be considered as unaffected, though, correctly speaking, it is slowly undergoing change.

A new idea intruding itself among old ones will probably meet with resistance from them—a resistance often arising in part from their philosophical nature, and in part from material interests that may have gathered round them. Its progress is, however, facilitated by that innate tendency to a change of thought which affects all men; for that in every individual there is a tendency to such a continuous variation of thought, no one can doubt who examines his own mental state at periods separated by a few years, and compares it with that of other persons examined at like epochs. The change observed in each is common to all, even though some may perhaps manifest it in a manner less conspicuous than others. The generality of the fact indicates that it originates in conditions to which all are subject; and that in nations there is a similar progression, may be readily proved by a superficial examination of their social state. In the progress of human affairs there arise classes of men who through their interests are identified with existing forms of opinion, and who manifest an extreme jealousy of any divergence from those forms. At first, because of the strength of public opinion coinciding with them and the feebleness of the commencing dissent, that jealousy may be gratified in open and violent persecution; but as the force of coinciding public opinion gradually declines, and the divergence or dissent gathers power, though the opposition may be none the less bitter, it is obliged to act in a more masked or insidious way. Eventually, through the continued operation of the same causes, even such indirect action ceases.

Many illustrations of these principles might be given, but one will suffice: it is the manner in which astronomical ideas have forced their way. Considering the probable consequences that might arise from the establishment of the Copernican system, particularly as respects the relative insignificance of our earth among such countless myriads of worlds, very many of which, by their size and importance, seem to be of inconceivably greater worth—considering the incompatibility of such views with the notion generally held in the Middle Ages that the universe was made for man, that its object and aim were altogether subordinate to human interests, it could not be otherwise than that opposition to so dangerous a divergency of thought should arise. Accordingly, it showed itself in the first period in a violent manner, seeking to extinguish the apparent heresy by the personal destruction or persecution of those who had fallen into it. But this by degrees passed away, and more moderate though more insidious methods were adopted. After a few years that opposition ceased. It is by no means the least interesting feature of these events that so great a resistance was thus successfully overcome, not alone against ancient authority, but even, as it were, against common sense; for he who adopts the philosophical doctrine of the globular figure of the earth, and assigns to it its true place as a member of the solar system, must question the evidence of his own eyes in matters that seem so incontestible as the rising and setting of the sun, and the actual effect of immense mountain ranges and great valleys in disturbing that globular form.

Whenever we see force applied for the controlling of ideas, whether it be in an open or in an indirect way, we may be sure that it is because material interests are in jeopardy, and that the power of the opinions on which they depend is becoming weak, and they themselves approaching to their end.

This example may also serve as an illustration of the manner in which the minds of men tend to unity of opinion in cases where knowledge of absolute truth is attainable, though they may be under very diverse interests. This, indeed, is the characteristic of exact science, that it spontaneously compels such a uniformity. In a question of arithmetic, no one contends against the true solution, though his personal interests may be opposed to it. In questions of geometry, neither the steps of the demonstration nor the conclusions are ever disputed, and the same holds good in questions of physics. Once let the true solution be reached, and it spontaneously compels universal assent. The exact solution of any such question, no matter what its bearing may be, forthwith becomes an undisputed rule of action, from which no person, if even he had the wish, could ever free himself. In the anarchy of opinion now prevailing on many points of interest to the well-being of society, this gives confidence to the hopes of the philosopher, for he sees that, year by year, the dominion of reason is spreading, and that men deliver themselves unreservedly to it; he sees that the essential weakness of many old forms of opinion was, in a great measure, attributable to this, that they led to a division of society into two unequal classes—a small one, which set itself above reason, and an immensely large one, which was beneath reason; the former outraging truth by the most audacious inventions for deceiving the latter, who, on their part, were the more completely duped the more transparent and preposterous the fraud. The one stood aloof from Reason because it was unsuited to their practices, the other declined it because it was inconsistent with their credulity. Institutions founded on such a state of things can have no innate strength, and only continue through the dexterous application of shifting expedients. But very different is it when men, instead of depreciating and distrusting Reason, put themselves unreservedly under its control: thence must arise unanimity, and unanimity is strength.

To the bar of common sense must be brought all ideas, whatsoever they may be, to receive their final judgment; and this, not only as respects those that are of a physical, but also those of a moral kind. There is no other course for it now in the world. Reason offers the only authority which men of all nations will acknowledge. Indeed, it is the recognition of this axiom which leads the European to the expectation that all other people will eventually adopt his faith, in view of the strong evidences he can present to them of its truth, and the unreasonableness of the ideas which they and their ancestors have followed; but what else is this than the exaltation of Reason above Authority? What other interpretation can we give of the numerous apologies and arguments put forth in their day by the different forms of faith? Are they not all essentially based upon the principle that Reason is the only, and must be the final judge?—that supernatural testimony must wait upon her decisions, and that faith is only sure when it is founded on common sense? How otherwise than upon this principle can we hope to bring the Buddhist and the Mohammedan from their fallacies—fallacies which at this moment are beguiling the greater part of the human race?

What I have just said respecting the modifications an idea must undergo through its collision with other ideas may be generalized. Entire systems of philosophy are liable to similar effects. They are nothing but modes of thought; and when they intrude themselves among dissimilar modes of thought, mutual displacements and alterations must ensue. The expectations of those who look forward to a glorious career for all nations of the earth in common, each catching a share of the enthusiasm and each contributing a share to the advance, are founded upon the effect which they suppose must ensue from the diffusion of our own power and enlightenment. What, they exclaim, will be the grand result, when our knowledge and ideas have become the common property of the world! What will it be when, by the printing-press, the telegraph, and other modern appliances, all men are brought in close interconnection, and, indeed, in instantaneous intercommunication! I would ask them to observe, for it is true that we stand on the brink of those events, what was the result to the ancient Greek philosophies, when, after the rise of Athens to political supremacy, they were all mingled together and compared together. Was it not the total destruction of them all? Brought into contact, as it were, at a common central point, none could gain an absolute predominance over all the rest. I would also ask them to look at the result of the supremacy of Rome—of her policy of patronizing all the forms of Paganism, and bringing them at one point in contact: again, was it not the utter destruction of them all? And so it must be when European systems of thought come into contact and conflict with Asiatic, as they will before long do, by the increasing means of intercommunication, which are in reality equivalent to centralization: each will no longer be measured by its own partial standard, but all must be submitted to that of a more general—nay, even of a universal kind. From such a conflict I do not believe that any would come forth without at least exhibiting marks of the most profound modification; and for the weaker Asiatic there seems to be no other issue than absolute destruction for all those parts that are not intrinsically true.

The American political system is founded on the principle of public intellectual culture. Recognizing the truth of the maxim that ideas govern the world, it rests its hopes on universal education. In this respect it differs essentially from its European contemporaries. They furnish enlightenment to certain classes only, not to the lower social strata.

Such a repressive policy can, however, never impart intrinsic strength to a community, as those who devised and those who adopted it supposed. The insecurity of Europe, whose civilization hangs over an awful gulf, and the strength of America, whose development is proceeding with so much energy, are each due to the course that has been followed in this respect. In Europe men grope about in political darkness, not knowing whither they are going, and afraid to look into the future. In America, the sentiment of a manifest destiny to imperial greatness gives to every one a determinate direction and an energetic life.

While the Slave States existed as a political power, they were forced by the necessities of their position to adopt the European maxim, and impose a forced ignorance on the low elements of their society. Had they done otherwise, the spark of enlightenment would quickly have kindled into a volcanic, devouring flame. But, since their overthrow in the Civil War, maxims of a very different, an opposite kind—those that have given such unparalleled power to the East, the North, the West—will come into play. There will be a harmony of action over the whole continent.

Intellectual development necessarily implies centralization; but, as we have seen in the foregoing pages, centralization is not incompatible with self-government; in fact, it may be the logical issue of democratic principles. It is through the working of this great truth that the Republic has passed through its inferior stage of life—the epoch of state sovereignties. At that time it was in the condition of one of those animated forms that have a dozen or more different nerve centres, each acting independently of the rest, or joining in concert only as suited itself, and hardly acknowledging the power of any central governing organ. But, as in animated nature and in individual man concentration accompanies development, so in national life there is an inevitable tendency to convergence, and to the conferring on a predetermined part a dominant control.

The practical working of these principles may be very advantageously studied in the pages of ecclesiastical history, which furnishes a lesson deserving the attention of every American — a beacon that may guide in the right path, that may warn from error. The first Christian communities established in Syria, Asia Minor, and elsewhere throughout the Roman Empire, present many highly interesting social analogies to the first American colonies. Their churches were the only political embodiments that were permissible or possible, and of them the constitution was essentially democratic, power being diffused in the congregation. The independent existence they maintained was by degrees modified, church affiliating with church, gathering thereby protection and conferring power. The individual helplessness they at first exhibited was exchanged for security. In a very short time, as concentration and centralization went on, a ruling personage emerged from among his clerical peers, who, passing into subordination, acknowledged his authority. The same tendency still unceasingly continuing, the bishops, in their turn, permitted a superior. In the time of Constantine, so completely had this process of centralization gone on, that power was ready to converge into the three great sees of Rome, Constantinople, Alexandria. Then came the struggle between them for supremacy. The annals of Europe for many years are its history. Eventually, the Bishop of Rome became the paramount authority over all.

There are but two elements of government—Faith

and Force. During the greater portion of its civilized life, Europe has been under the dominion of the former. For many centuries its kings were nothing more than lieutenants of the Sovereign Pontiff. In assigning, as we so commonly do, a superiority to the political over the ecclesiastical element in the history of that continent, we fall into a misapprehension: we adopt the views of those who consider only the integrant or constituent states, and not the view that ought to be adopted from a contemplation of their aggregate—the continent; for there was a time, a long time, in which ecclesiasticism discharged those international relationships that are now discharged by diplomacy. In Rome resided the animating, the uniting principle of all.

Those Christian Congresses that pass under the designation of Councils are not without their analogues in the American political system. To us there can be nothing more interesting than to study their relations with the executive Papal authority—how it called them into action when its purposes required, and how, when its statesmanship indicated, it evaded or declined to permit their continued existence. How different the result, had a Senate of Christendom been possible—a supreme authoritative body, with the Pope as its first executive officer! There were often great men who saw that that was the chief necessity of their times; there were Councils that attempted to accomplish it.

In the history of this wonderful power, that for a thousand years maintained its sway, the American, I repeat, may find abundant instruction. Only let him divest his mind of the impression that there was any thing supernatural about it, for that serves to diminish its intrinsic merit as the most extraordinary and most successful of human political conceptions carried into practical operation. He may realize from it the inevitable course through which all enduring human associations must pass. He may see how, in its limited sphere, it depended on the same principles on which he is depending. It signified nothing to the Church that her greatest dignitaries had come from the lowest social ranks. Mental capacity was what she sought; she appropriated it wherever she could find it. Considering the intrinsic weakness of the intellectual basis on which she rested, considering how incompatible it was with increasing enlightenment, our admiration may be worthily excited by the wondrous duration of her power. In that we may perceive auspices of the most favorable kind for ourselves, who likewise are making every thing depend on the organization of intellect; not, however, as she did, for securing the stability of what, at the most, was only an institution, but for a nation; not resting ourselves, as she did, on the supernatural, which is in its very nature delusive and unsatisfactory, but on Reason, which is enduring. Italian ecclesiasticism was necessarily a specialty; American republicanism is for a continent. The one was mainly concerned in perpetuating the power of a guild; the other is intended indiscriminately for all classes of men. But a philosophical study of the political history of the former—its transcendent successes as well as its conspicuous misfortunes—the course of events through which it passed—the profound knowledge it displayed of men, and, it may be emphatically added, of women too, who constitute a most important element of national life—the modes of action it observed toward antagonizing influences—its equanimity in the meridian splendor of its power—its tenacity of purpose, as inexorable as the grave in adversity—these are things which we, who are commencing a career of grandeur in a parallel direction, also requiring democratic principles to be co-ordinated with self-government, and that with organization of intellect and concentration of power, may find to be worthy of our most profound attention.

# INDEX.

THE END.

ANNUAL RECORD OF SCIENCE AND INDUSTRY FOR 1872. Edited by Prof. SPENCER F. BAIRD, of the Smithsonian Institution, with the Assistance of Eminent Men of Science. 12mo, over 700 pp., Cloth, $2 00. (Uniform with the *Annual Record of Science and Industry for* 1871. 12mo, Cloth, $2 00.)

COL. FORNEY'S ANECDOTES OF PUBLIC MEN. Anecdotes of Public Men. By JOHN W. FORNEY. 12mo, Cloth, $2 00.

MISS BEECHER'S HOUSEKEEPER AND HEALTHKEEPER: Containing Five Hundred Recipes for Economical and Healthful Cooking; also, many Directions for securing Health and Happiness. Approved by Physicians of all Classes. Illustrations. 12mo, Cloth, $1 50.

FARM BALLADS. By WILL CARLETON. Handsomely Illustrated. Square 8vo, Ornamental Cloth, $2 00; Gilt Edges, $2 50.

POETS OF THE NINETEENTH CENTURY. The Poets of the Nineteenth Century. Selected and Edited by the Rev. ROBERT ARIS WILLMOTT. With English and American Additions, arranged by EVERT A. DUYCKINCK, Editor of "Cyclopædia of American Literature." Comprising Selections from the Greatest Authors of the Age. Superbly Illustrated with 141 Engravings from Designs by the most Eminent Artists. In elegant small 4to form, printed on Superfine Tinted Paper, richly bound in extra Cloth, Beveled, Gilt Edges, $5 00; Half Calf, $5 50; Full Turkey Morocco, $9 00.

THE REVISION OF THE ENGLISH VERSION OF THE NEW TESTAMENT. With an Introduction by the Rev. P. SCHAFF, D.D. 618 pp., Crown 8vo, Cloth, $3 00.

This work embraces in one volume:

I. ON A FRESH REVISION OF THE ENGLISH NEW TESTAMENT. By J. B. LIGHTFOOT, D.D., Canon of St. Paul's, and Hulsean Professor of Divinity, Cambridge. Second Edition, Revised. 196 pp.

II. ON THE AUTHORIZED VERSION OF THE NEW TESTAMENT in Connection with some Recent Proposals for its Revision. By RICHARD CHENEVIX TRENCH, D.D., Archbishop of Dublin. 194 pp.

III. CONSIDERATIONS ON THE REVISION OF THE ENGLISH VERSION OF THE NEW TESTAMENT. By C. J. ELLICOTT, D.D., Bishop of Gloucester and Bristol. 178 pp.

NORDHOFF'S CALIFORNIA. California: For Health, Pleasure, and Residence. A Book for Travelers and Settlers. Illustrated. 8vo, Paper, $2 00; Cloth, $2 50.

MOTLEY'S DUTCH REPUBLIC. The Rise of the Dutch Republic. By JOHN LOTHROP MOTLEY, LL.D., D.C.L. With a Portrait of William of Orange. 3 vols., 8vo, Cloth, $10 50.

MOTLEY'S UNITED NETHERLANDS. History of the United Netherlands: from the Death of William the Silent to the Twelve Years' Truce—1609. With a full View of the English-Dutch Struggle against Spain, and of the Origin and Destruction of the Spanish Armada. By JOHN LOTHROP MOTLEY, LL.D., D.C.L. Portraits. 4 vols., 8vo, Cloth, $14 00.

NAPOLEON'S LIFE OF CÆSAR. The History of Julius Cæsar. By His late Imperial Majesty NAPOLEON III. Two Volumes ready. Library Edition, 8vo, Cloth, $3 50 per vol.

HAYDN'S DICTIONARY OF DATES, relating to all Ages and Nations. For Universal Reference. Edited by BENJAMIN VINCENT, Assistant Secretary and Keeper of the Library of the Royal Institution of Great Britain; and Revised for the Use of American Readers. 8vo, Cloth, $5 00; Sheep, $6 00.

MACGREGOR'S ROB ROY ON THE JORDAN. The Rob Roy on the Jordan, Nile, Red Sea, and Gennesareth, &c. A Canoe Cruise in Palestine and Egypt, and the Waters of Damascus. By J. MACGREGOR, M.A. With Maps and Illustrations. Crown 8vo, Cloth, $2 50.

**WALLACE'S MALAY ARCHIPELAGO.** The Malay Archipelago: the Land of the Orang-Utan and the Bird of Paradise. A Narrative of Travel, 1854–1862. With Studies of Man and Nature. By ALFRED RUSSEL WALLACE. With Ten Maps and Fifty-one Elegant Illustrations. Crown 8vo, Cloth, $2 50.

**WHYMPER'S ALASKA.** Travel and Adventure in the Territory of Alaska, formerly Russian America—now Ceded to the United States—and in various other parts of the North Pacific. By FREDERICK WHYMPER With Map and Illustrations. Crown 8vo, Cloth, $2 50.

**ORTON'S ANDES AND THE AMAZON.** The Andes and the Amazon; or, Across the Continent of South America. By JAMES ORTON, M.A., Professor of Natural History in Vassar College, Poughkeepsie, N. Y., and Corresponding Member of the Academy of Natural Sciences, Philadelphia. With a New Map of Equatorial America and numerous Illustrations. Crown 8vo, Cloth, $2 00.

**WINCHELL'S SKETCHES OF CREATION.** Sketches of Creation: a Popular View of some of the Grand Conclusions of the Sciences in reference to the History of Matter and of Life. Together with a Statement of the Intimations of Science respecting the Primordial Condition and the Ultimate Destiny of the Earth and the Solar System. By ALEXANDER WINCHELL, LL.D., Chancellor of the Syracuse University. With Illustrations. 12mo, Cloth, $2 00.

**WHITE'S MASSACRE OF ST. BARTHOLOMEW.** The Massacre of St. Bartholomew: Preceded by a History of the Religious Wars in the Reign of Charles IX. By HENRY WHITE, M.A. With Illustrations. 8vo, Cloth, $1 75.

**LOSSING'S FIELD-BOOK OF THE REVOLUTION.** Pictorial Field-Book of the Revolution; or, Illustrations, by Pen and Pencil, of the History, Biography, Scenery, Relics, and Traditions of the War for Independence. By BENSON J. LOSSING. 2 vols., 8vo, Cloth, $14 00; Sheep, $15 00; Half Calf, $18 00; Full Turkey Morocco, $22 00.

**LOSSING'S FIELD-BOOK OF THE WAR OF 1812.** Pictorial Field-Book of the War of 1812; or, Illustrations, by Pen and Pencil, of the History, Biography, Scenery, Relics, and Traditions of the Last War for American Independence. By BENSON J. LOSSING. With several hundred Engravings on Wood, by Lossing and Barritt, chiefly from Original Sketches by the Author. 1088 pages, 8vo, Cloth, $7 00; Sheep, $8 50; Half Calf, $10 00.

**ALFORD'S GREEK TESTAMENT.** The Greek Testament: with a critically revised Text; a Digest of Various Readings; Marginal References to Verbal and Idiomatic Usage; Prolegomena; and a Critical and Exegetical Commentary. For the Use of Theological Students and Ministers. By HENRY ALFORD, D.D., Dean of Canterbury. Vol. I., containing the Four Gospels. 944 pages, 8vo, Cloth, $6 00; Sheep, $6 50.

**ABBOTT'S FREDERICK THE GREAT.** The History of Frederick the Second, called Frederick the Great. By JOHN S. C. ABBOTT. Elegantly Illustrated. 8vo, Cloth, $5 00.

**ABBOTT'S HISTORY OF THE FRENCH REVOLUTION.** The French Revolution of 1789, as viewed in the Light of Republican Institutions. By JOHN S. C. ABBOTT. With 100 Engravings. 8vo, Cloth, $5 00.

**ABBOTT'S NAPOLEON BONAPARTE.** The History of Napoleon Bonaparte. By JOHN S. C. ABBOTT. With Maps, Woodcuts, and Portraits on Steel. 2 vols., 8vo, Cloth, $10 00.

**ABBOTT'S NAPOLEON AT ST. HELENA;** or, Interesting Anecdotes and Remarkable Conversations of the Emperor during the Five and a Half Years of his Captivity. Collected from the Memorials of Las Casas, O'Meara, Montholon, Antommarchi, and others. By JOHN S. C. ABBOTT. With Illustrations. 8vo, Cloth, $5 00.

**ADDISON'S COMPLETE WORKS.** The Works of Joseph Addison, embracing the whole of the "Spectator." Complete in 3 vols., 8vo, Cloth, $6 00.

ALCOCK'S JAPAN. The Capital of the Tycoon: a Narrative of a Three Years' Residence in Japan. By Sir RUTHERFORD ALCOCK, K.C.B., Her Majesty's Envoy Extraordinary and Minister Plenipotentiary in Japan With Maps and Engravings. 2 vols., 12mo, Cloth, $3 50.

ALISON'S HISTORY OF EUROPE. FIRST SERIES: From the Commencement of the French Revolution, in 1789, to the Restoration of the Bourbons, in 1815. [In addition to the Notes on Chapter LXXVI., which correct the errors of the original work concerning the United States, a copious Analytical Index has been appended to this American Edition.] SECOND SERIES: From the Fall of Napoleon, in 1815, to the Accession of Louis Napoleon, in 1852. 8 vols., 8vo, Cloth, $16 00.

BARTH'S NORTH AND CENTRAL AFRICA. Travels and Discoveries in North and Central Africa: being a Journal of an Expedition undertaken under the Auspices of H.B.M.'s Government, in the Years 1849–1855. By HENRY BARTH, Ph.D., D.C.L. Illustrated. 3 vols., 8vo, Cloth, $12 00.

HENRY WARD BEECHER'S SERMONS. Sermons by HENRY WARD BEECHER, Plymouth Church, Brooklyn. Selected from Published and Unpublished Discourses, and Revised by their Author. With Steel Portrait. Complete in 2 vols., 8vo, Cloth, $5 00.

LYMAN BEECHER'S AUTOBIOGRAPHY, &c. Autobiography, Correspondence, &c., of Lyman Beecher, D.D. Edited by his Son, CHARLES BEECHER. With Three Steel Portraits, and Engravings on Wood. In 2 vols., 12mo, Cloth, $5 00.

BOSWELL'S JOHNSON. The Life of Samuel Johnson, LL.D. Including a Journey to the Hebrides. By JAMES BOSWELL, Esq. A New Edition, with numerous Additions and Notes. By JOHN WILSON CROKER, LL.D., F.R.S. Portrait of Boswell. 2 vols., 8vo, Cloth, $4 00.

DRAPER'S CIVIL WAR. History of the American Civil War. By JOHN W. DRAPER, M.D., LL.D., Professor of Chemistry and Physiology in the University of New York. In Three Vols. 8vo, Cloth, $3 50 per vol.

DRAPER'S INTELLECTUAL DEVELOPMENT OF EUROPE. A History of the Intellectual Development of Europe. By JOHN W. DRAPER, M.D., LL.D., Professor of Chemistry and Physiology in the University of New York. 8vo, Cloth, $5 00.

DRAPER'S AMERICAN CIVIL POLICY. Thoughts on the Future Civil Policy of America. By JOHN W. DRAPER, M.D., LL.D., Professor of Chemistry and Physiology in the University of New York. Crown 8vo, Cloth, $2 50.

DU CHAILLU'S AFRICA. Explorations and Adventures in Equatorial Africa, with Accounts of the Manners and Customs of the People, and of the Chase of the Gorilla, the Crocodile, Leopard, Elephant, Hippopotamus, and other Animals. By PAUL B. DU CHAILLU. Numerous Illustrations. 8vo, Cloth, $5 00.

DU CHAILLU'S ASHANGO LAND. A Journey to Ashango Land: and Further Penetration into Equatorial Africa. By PAUL B. DU CHAILLU. New Edition. Handsomely Illustrated. 8vo, Cloth, $5 00.

BELLOWS'S OLD WORLD. The Old World in its New Face: Impressions of Europe in 1867–1868. By HENRY W. BELLOWS. 2 vols., 12mo, Cloth, $3 50.

BRODHEAD'S HISTORY OF NEW YORK. History of the State of New York. By JOHN ROMEYN BRODHEAD. 1609–1691. 2 vols. 8vo, Cloth, $3 00 per vol.

BROUGHAM'S AUTOBIOGRAPHY. Life and Times of HENRY, LORD BROUGHAM. Written by Himself. In Three Volumes. 12mo, Cloth, $2 00 per vol.

BULWER'S PROSE WORKS. Miscellaneous Prose Works of Edward Bulwer, Lord Lytton. 2 vols., 12mo, Cloth, $3 50.

BULWER'S HORACE. The Odes and Epodes of Horace. A Metrical Translation into English. With Introduction and Commentaries. By LORD LYTTON. With Latin Text from the Editions of Orelli, Macleane, and Yonge. 12mo, Cloth, $1 75.

BULWER'S KING ARTHUR, A Poem. By LORD LYTTON. New Edition. 12mo, Cloth, $1 75.

BURNS'S LIFE AND WORKS. The Life and Works of Robert Burns. Edited by ROBERT CHAMBERS. 4 vols., 12mo, Cloth, $6 00.

REINDEER, DOGS, AND SNOW-SHOES. A Journal of Siberian Travel and Explorations made in the Years 1865–'67. By RICHARD J. BUSH, late of the Russo-American Telegraph Expedition. Illustrated. Crown 8vo, Cloth, $3 00.

CARLYLE'S FREDERICK THE GREAT. History of Friedrich II., called Frederick the Great. By THOMAS CARLYLE. Portraits, Maps, Plans, &c. 6 vols., 12mo, Cloth, $12 00.

CARLYLE'S FRENCH REVOLUTION. History of the French Revolution. 2 vols., 12mo, Cloth, $3 50.

CARLYLE'S OLIVER CROMWELL. Letters and Speeches of Oliver Cromwell. With Elucidations and Connecting Narrative. 2 vols., 12mo, Cloth, $3 50.

CHALMERS'S POSTHUMOUS WORKS. The Posthumous Works of Dr. Chalmers. Edited by his Son-in-Law, Rev. WILLIAM HANNA, LL.D. Complete in 9 vols., 12mo, Cloth, $13 50.

COLERIDGE'S COMPLETE WORKS. The Complete Works of Samuel Taylor Coleridge. With an Introductory Essay upon his Philosophical and Theological Opinions. Edited by Professor SHEDD. Complete in Seven Vols. With a Portrait. Small 8vo, Cloth, $10 50.

DOOLITTLE'S CHINA. Social Life of the Chinese: with some Account of their Religious, Governmental, Educational, and Business Customs and Opinions. With special but not exclusive Reference to Fuhchau. By Rev. JUSTUS DOOLITTLE, Fourteen Years Member of the Fuhchau Mission of the American Board. Illustrated with more that 150 characteristic Engravings on Wood. 2 vols., 12mo, Cloth, $5 00.

GIBBON'S ROME. History of the Decline and Fall of the Roman Empire. By EDWARD GIBBON. With Notes by Rev. H. H. MILMAN and M. GUIZOT. A new cheap Edition. To which is added a complete Index of the whole Work, and a Portrait of the Author. 6 vols., 12mo, Cloth, $9 00.

HAZEN'S SCHOOL AND ARMY IN GERMANY AND FRANCE. The School and the Army in Germany and France, with a Diary of Siege Life at Versailles. By Brevet Major-General W. B. HAZEN, U.S.A., Colonel Sixth Infantry. Crown 8vo, Cloth, $2 50.

HARPER'S NEW CLASSICAL LIBRARY. Literal Translations.

The following Vols. are now ready. 12mo, Cloth, $1 50 each.

CÆSAR.—VIRGIL.—SALLUST.—HORACE.—CICERO'S ORATIONS.—CICERO'S OFFICES, &C.—CICERO ON ORATORY AND ORATORS.—TACITUS (2 vols.).—TERENCE.—SOPHOCLES.—JUVENAL.—XENOPHON.—HOMER'S ILIAD.—HOMER'S ODYSSEY.—HERODOTUS.—DEMOSTHENES.—THUCYDIDES.—ÆSCHYLUS.—EURIPIDES (2 vols.).—LIVY (2 vols.).

DAVIS'S CARTHAGE. Carthage and her Remains: being an Account of the Excavations and Researches on the Site of the Phœnician Metropolis in Africa and other adjacent Places. Conducted under the Auspices of Her Majesty's Government. By Dr. DAVIS, F.R.G.S. Profusely Illustrated with Maps, Woodcuts, Chromo-Lithographs, &c. 8vo, Cloth, $4 00.

EDGEWORTH'S (MISS) NOVELS. With Engravings. 10 vols., 12mo, Cloth, $15 00.

GROTE'S HISTORY OF GREECE. 12 vols., 12mo, Cloth, $18 00.

HELPS'S SPANISH CONQUEST. The Spanish Conquest in America, and its Relation to the History of Slavery and to the Government of Colonies. By ARTHUR HELPS. 4 vols., 12mo, Cloth, $6 00.

HALE'S (MRS.) WOMAN'S RECORD. Woman's Record; or, Biographical Sketches of all Distinguished Women, from the Creation to the Present Time. Arranged in Four Eras, with Selections from Female Writers of Each Era. By Mrs. SARAH JOSEPHA HALE. Illustrated with more than 200 Portraits. 8vo, Cloth, $5 00.

HALL'S ARCTIC RESEARCHES. Arctic Researches and Life among the Esquimaux: being the Narrative of an Expedition in Search of Sir John Franklin, in the Years 1860, 1861, and 1862. By CHARLES FRANCIS HALL. With Maps and 100 Illustrations. The Illustrations are from the Original Drawings by Charles Parsons, Henry L. Stephens, Solomon Eytinge, W. S. L. Jewett, and Granville Perkins, after Sketches by Captain Hall. 8vo, Cloth, $5 00.

HALLAM'S CONSTITUTIONAL HISTORY OF ENGLAND, from the Accession of Henry VII. to the Death of George II. 8vo, Cloth, $2 00.

HALLAM'S LITERATURE. Introduction to the Literature of Europe during the Fifteenth, Sixteenth, and Seventeenth Centuries. By HENRY HALLAM. 2 vols., 8vo, Cloth, $4 00.

HALLAM'S MIDDLE AGES. State of Europe during the Middle Ages. By HENRY HALLAM. 8vo, Cloth, $2 00.

HILDRETH'S HISTORY OF THE UNITED STATES. FIRST SERIES: From the First Settlement of the Country to the Adoption of the Federal Constitution. SECOND SERIES: From the Adoption of the Federal Constitution to the End of the Sixteenth Congress. 6 vols., 8vo, Cloth, $18 00.

HUME'S HISTORY OF ENGLAND. History of England, from the Invasion of Julius Cæsar to the Abdication of James II., 1688. By DAVID HUME. A new Edition, with the Author's last Corrections and Improvements. To which is Prefixed a short Account of his Life, written by Himself. With a Portrait of the Author. 6 vols., 12mo, Cloth, $9 00.

JAY'S WORKS. Complete Works of Rev. William Jay: comprising his Sermons, Family Discourses, Morning and Evening Exercises for every Day in the Year, Family Prayers, &c. Author's enlarged Edition, revised. 3 vols., 8vo, Cloth, $6 00.

JEFFERSON'S DOMESTIC LIFE. The Domestic Life of Thomas Jefferson: compiled from Family Letters and Reminiscences, by his Great-Granddaughter, SARAH N. RANDOLPH. With Illustrations. Crown 8vo, Illuminated Cloth, Beveled Edges, $2 50.

JOHNSON'S COMPLETE WORKS. The Works of Samuel Johnson, LL.D. With an Essay on his Life and Genius, by ARTHUR MURPHY, Esq. Portrait of Johnson. 2 vols., 8vo, Cloth, $4 00.

KINGLAKE'S CRIMEAN WAR. The Invasion of the Crimea, and an Account of its Progress down to the Death of Lord Raglan. By ALEXANDER WILLIAM KINGLAKE. With Maps and Plans. Two Vols. ready. 12mo, Cloth, $2 00 per vol.

KINGSLEY'S WEST INDIES. At Last: A Christmas in the West Indies. By CHARLES KINGSLEY. Illustrated. 12mo, Cloth, $1 50.

KRUMMACHER'S DAVID, KING OF ISRAEL. David, the King of Israel: a Portrait drawn from Bible History and the Book of Psalms. By FREDERICK WILLIAM KRUMMACHER, D.D., Author of "Elijah the Tishbite," &c. Translated under the express Sanction of the Author by the Rev. M. G. EASTON, M.A. With a Letter from Dr. Krummacher to his American Readers, and a Portrait. 12mo, Cloth, $1 75.

LAMB'S COMPLETE WORKS. The Works of Charles Lamb. Comprising his Letters, Poems, Essays of Elia, Essays upon Shakspeare, Hogarth, &c., and a Sketch of his Life, with the Final Memorials, by T. NOON TALFOURD. Portrait. 2 vols., 12mo, Cloth, $3 00.

LIVINGSTONE'S SOUTH AFRICA. Missionary Travels and Researches in South Africa; including a Sketch of Sixteen Years' Residence in the Interior of Africa, and a Journey from the Cape of Good Hope to Loando on the West Coast; thence across the Continent, down the River Zambesi, to the Eastern Ocean. By DAVID LIVINGSTONE, LL.D., D.C.L. With Portrait, Maps by Arrowsmith, and numerous Illustrations. 8vo, Cloth, $4 50.

LIVINGSTONES' ZAMBESI. Narrative of an Expedition to the Zambesi and its Tributaries, and of the Discovery of the Lakes Shirwa and Nyassa. 1858–1864. By DAVID and CHARLES LIVINGSTONE. With Map and Illustrations. 8vo, Cloth, $5 00.

M'CLINTOCK & STRONG'S CYCLOPÆDIA. Cyclopædia of Biblical, Theological, and Ecclesiastical Literature. Prepared by the Rev. JOHN M'CLINTOCK, D.D., and JAMES STRONG, S.T.D. *5 vols. now ready.* Royal 8vo, Price per vol., Cloth, $5 00; Sheep, $6 00; Half Morocco, $8 00.

MARCY'S ARMY LIFE ON THE BORDER. Thirty Years of Army Life on the Border. Comprising descriptions of the Indian Nomads of the Plains; Explorations of New Territory; a Trip across the Rocky Mountains in the Winter; Descriptions of the Habits of Different Animals found in the West, and the Methods of Hunting them; with Incidents in the Life of Different Frontier Men, &c., &c. By Brevet Brigadier-General R. B. MARCY, U.S.A., Author of "The Prairie Traveller." With numerous Illustrations. 8vo, Cloth, Beveled Edges, $3 00.

MACAULAY'S HISTORY OF ENGLAND. The History of England from the Accession of James II. By THOMAS BABINGTON MACAULAY. With an Original Portrait of the Author. 5 vols., 8vo, Cloth, $10 00; 12mo, Cloth, $7 50.

MOSHEIM'S ECCLESIASTICAL HISTORY, Ancient and Modern; in which the Rise, Progress, and Variation of Church Power are considered in their Connection with the State of Learning and Philosophy, and the Political History of Europe during that Period. Translated, with Notes, &c., by A. MACLAINE, D.D. A new Edition, continued to 1826, by C. COOTE, LL.D. 2 vols., 8vo, Cloth, $4 00.

THE DESERT OF THE EXODUS. Journeys on Foot in the Wilderness of the Forty Years' Wanderings; undertaken in connection with the Ordnance Survey of Sinai and the Palestine Exploration Fund. By E. H. PALMER, M.A., Lord Almoner's Professor of Arabic, and Fellow of St. John's College, Cambridge. With Maps and numerous Illustrations from Photographs and Drawings taken on the spot by the Sinai Survey Expedition and C. F. Tyrwhitt Drake. Crown 8vo, Cloth, $3 00.

OLIPHANT'S CHINA AND JAPAN. Narrative of the Earl of Elgin's Mission to China and Japan, in the Years 1857, '58, '59. By LAURENCE OLIPHANT, Private Secretary to Lord Elgin. Illustrations. 8vo, Cloth, $3 50.

OLIPHANT'S (MRS.) LIFE OF EDWARD IRVING. The Life of Edward Irving, Minister of the National Scotch Church, London. Illustrated by his Journals and Correspondence. By Mrs. OLIPHANT. Portrait. 8vo, Cloth, $3 50.

RAWLINSON'S MANUAL OF ANCIENT HISTORY. A Manual of Ancient History, from the Earliest Times to the Fall of the Western Empire. Comprising the History of Chaldæa, Assyria, Media, Babylonia, Lydia, Phœnicia, Syria, Judæa, Egypt, Carthage, Persia, Greece, Macedonia, Parthia, and Rome. By GEORGE RAWLINSON, M.A., Camden Professor of Ancient History in the University of Oxford. 12mo, Cloth, $2 50.

RECLUS'S THE EARTH. The Earth: A Descriptive History of the Phenomena and Life of the Globe. By ÉLISÉE RECLUS. Translated by the late B. B. Woodward, and Edited by Henry Woodward. With 234 Maps and Illustrations and 23 Page Maps printed in Colors. 8vo, Cloth, $5 00.

RECLUS'S OCEAN. The Ocean, Atmosphere, and Life. Being the Second Series of a Descriptive History of the Life of the Globe. By ÉLISÉE RECLUS. Profusely Illustrated with 250 Maps or Figures, and 27 Maps printed in Colors. 8vo, Cloth, $6 00.

SHAKSPEARE. The Dramatic Works of William Shakspeare, with the Corrections and Illustrations of Dr. JOHNSON, G. STEVENS, and others. Revised by ISAAC REED. Engravings. 6 vols, Royal 12mo, Cloth, $9 00. 2 vols., 8vo, Cloth, $4 00.

SMILES'S LIFE OF THE STEPHENSONS. The Life of George Stephenson, and of his Son, Robert Stephenson; comprising, also, a History of the Invention and Introduction of the Railway Locomotive. By SAMUEL SMILES, Author of "Self-Help," &c. With Steel Portraits and numerous Illustrations. 8vo, Cloth, $3 00.

SMILES'S HISTORY OF THE HUGUENOTS. The Huguenots: their Settlements, Churches, and Industries in England and Ireland. By SAMUEL SMILES. With an Appendix relating to the Huguenots in America. Crown 8vo, Cloth, $1 75.

SPEKE'S AFRICA. Journal of the Discovery of the Source of the Nile. By Captain JOHN HANNING SPEKE, Captain H.M. Indian Army, Fellow and Gold Medalist of the Royal Geographical Society, Hon. Corresponding Member and Gold Medalist of the French Geographical Society, &c. With Maps and Portraits and numerous Illustrations, chiefly from Drawings by Captain GRANT. 8vo, Cloth, uniform with Livingstone, Barth, Burton, &c., $4 00.

STRICKLAND'S (MISS) QUEENS OF SCOTLAND. Lives of the Queens of Scotland and English Princesses connected with the Regal Succession of Great Britain. Py AGNES STRICKLAND. 8 vols., 12mo, Cloth, $12 00.

THE STUDENT'S SERIES.
France. Engravings. 12mo, Cloth, $2 00.
Gibbon. Engravings. 12mo, Cloth, $2 00.
Greece. Engravings. 12mo, Cloth, $2 00.
Hume. Engravings. 12mo, Cloth, $2 00.
Rome. By Liddell. Engravings. 12mo, Cloth, $2 00.
Old Testament History. Engravings. 12mo, Cloth, $2 00.
New Testament History. Engravings, 12mo, Cloth, $2 00.
Strickland's Queens of England. Abridged. Eng's. 12mo, Cloth, $2 00.
Ancient History of the East. 12mo, Cloth, $2 00.
Hallam's Middle Ages. 12mo, Cloth, $2 00.
Hallam's Constitutional History of England. 12mo, Cloth, $2 00.
Lyell's Elements of Geology. 12mo, Cloth, $2 00.

TENNYSON'S COMPLETE POEMS. The Complete Poems of Alfred Tennyson, Poet Laureate. With numerous Illustrations by Eminent Artists, and Three Characteristic Portraits. 8vo, Paper, 75 cents; Cloth, $1 25.

THOMSON'S LAND AND THE BOOK. The Land and the Book; or, Biblical Illustrations drawn from the Manners and Customs, the Scenes and the Scenery of the Holy Land. By W. M. THOMSON, D.D., Twenty-five Years a Missionary of the A.B.C.F.M. in Syria and Palestine. With two elaborate Maps of Palestine, an accurate Plan of Jerusalem, and several hundred Engravings, representing the Scenery, Topography, and Productions of the Holy Land, and the Costumes, Manners, and Habits of the People. 2 large 12mo vols., Cloth, $5 00.

TYERMAN'S WESLEY. The Life and Times of the Rev. John Wesley, M.A., Founder of the Methodists. By the Rev. LUKE TYERMAN. Portraits. 3 vols., Crown 8vo, Cloth, $7 50.

TYERMAN'S OXFORD METHODISTS. The Oxford Methodists: Memoirs of the Rev. Messrs. Clayton, Ingham, Gambold, Hervey, and Broughton, with Biographical Notices of others. By the Rev. L. TYERMAN. With Portraits. Crown 8vo, Cloth, $2 50.

VÁMBÉRY'S CENTRAL ASIA. Travels in Central Asia. Being the Account of a Journey from Teheren across the Turkoman Desert, on the Eastern Shore of the Caspian, to Khiva, Bokhara, and Samarcand, performed in the Year 1863. By ARMINIUS VÁMBÉRY, Member of the Hungarian Academy of Pesth, by whom he was sent on this Scientific Mission. With Map and Woodcuts. 8vo, Cloth, $4 50.

WOOD'S HOMES WITHOUT HANDS. Homes Without Hands: being a Description of the Habitations of Animals, classed according to their Principle of Construction. By J. G. WOOD, M.A., F.L.S. With about 140 Illustrations. 8vo, Cloth, Beveled Edges, $4 50.

www.ingramcontent.com/pod-product-compliance
Lightning Source LLC
LaVergne TN
LVHW020216110826
845151LV00003B/739